Ƀ

TO THE

BASICS

Discipleship

Dr. James Wilkins

Milk of the Word
BOOK I

"Feed my Lambs" John 21:15

A Scriptural Follow-up
Program which works

Printed in the United States of America

21st Printing   5,000

Printed to date: 130,000

Printed by
Christian Services Network (CSN)
1975 Janich Ranch Road
El Cajon, CA 92019-1150
1-866-484-6184

DEDICATION

This book is lovingly dedicated to my wife, Louella, who for twenty-five years helped me nurse and develop the "LAMBS" which the Lord gave us in our ministry.

Together we would like to present this book to the pastors and to their churches in an effort to help conserve the results and develop THEIR LAMBS INTO FULL-GROWN SHEEP.

TABLE OF CONTENTS

PRESENTATION PAGE

YOUR BIRTHDAYS

This is presented to_____

Who was born into the physical realm on_____

                                                Month   Day   Year

In_____ _____ _____

      City   State   Zip

He was born into the Spiritual realm on _____ in

_____ _____ _____

      City   State   Zip

YOUR FAMILY RELATIONSHIPS

On _____ he became part of his domestic family.

    Month   Day   Year

His father, _____, was responsible

to God to develop him into a well adjusted, mature adult. On

_____, he became part of the _____

   Month   Day   Year

_____church family. The man whom God

appointed over him, to watch after his soul and fully develop

him, was Pastor _____Hebrews 13:17

YOUR BIG BROTHER RESPONSIBILITY

Your Big Brother/Sister's name is _____
his/her job is to assist the Pastor in helping you learn how to properly
feed yourself, so that you can grow spiritually and become a mature
child of God. Your job as a Christian is to strive to fulfill God's will
for your life, which is to be fruitful.

Your Big Brother/Sister's phone number is _____

SIMPLE STEPS IN USING THIS BOOK

1. The Pastor or Discipleship Director appoints a Role Model for you who has gone through these lessons.

2. The Role Model fills in the Presentation Page.

3. The Role Model meets with the new convert and introduces the book to him. He goes over the "Dear Disciple" letter and fills in the blanks on the Prayer List Page.

4. The Role Model goes over the Daily Declaration and explains how to do it each morning and evening.

5. The Role Model explains the grading procedure. He explains that the new member is to read each daily assignment on the day assigned for each part of his lesson before answering any of the questions.

6. Then he is to fill in the blanks on the day designated: Monday's on Monday, Tuesday's on Tuesday, etc.

7. Each week the Role Model sets up a visit for a Saturday or Sunday, at an appointed time, to fellowship, review, and go over the questions.

8. The Role Model assigns the proper grade to the lesson.

    A = Excellent: Did the work correctly on a daily basis.
    B = Good: Did all the work, but not on a daily basis.
    N = Needs prayer: Did not complete all the blanks.

9. The Role Model has prayer, leaves, and makes his report.

10. The same procedure is followed for each week's lesson.

DEAR DISCIPLE,

Isn't it thrilling to think of yourself as a DISCIPLE OF CHRIST? You have accepted Jesus as your saviour, and as commanded in II Peter 3:18, you are now in the process of growing in Grace and the Knowledge of our Lord Jesus Christ.

DID YOU KNOW...

That Jesus came into the world that you may have eternal life and have it more ABUNDANTLY? (John 10:10)

That Paul admonished his converts to be "strong in the Lord and the power of His might?" (Ephesians 6:10)

That God gave us the Holy Bible, so the child of God could be perfect (mature or full grown), and be completely furnished for every good work? (II Timothy 3:16-17)

This Book, "*Back to the Basics*" was written for you with the purpose that God had in mind for your life. God wants you, HIS LITTLE CHILD, to become A CHAMPION.

In order to become a champion in any area of life, one must submit to DISCIPLINE AND TRAINING. This book will give you the practical outline, exercise, and proper guidance, which will lead to a successful, abundant life.

Read the ascribed lesson, fill in the blanks EVERY DAY, and STRIVE TO MAKE AN "A."

Repeat the DAILY DECLARATION at least once every morning and evening.

Repeat the memory verse every morning and evening until you have memorized it.

We look at the early New Testament disciples with starry eyes and think of them as "Spiritual Giants" or "Heroes of the Faith." Yet, by following the simple steps outlined in this book, you will become a real Bible disciple in this 21st Century. God will use you to bless and help your family as He used the New Testament disciples 2,000 years ago.

Remember, Jesus said that when you pray, enter into thy closet and shut the door. Why? Because He wants the person not to be distracted as he prays aloud. On the following page, we have a sample for you to follow. When one prays aloud and knows he is praying properly, it will create real confidence and boldness in one's prayer life.

Congratulations and God bless you. Always remember, NOW YOU ARE HIS DISCIPLE, and you can expect Him to help you just as He helped the disciples who lived for Him in the Bible days.

Yours for Spiritual Growth,

James Wilkins

Dr. James Wilkins

How to Begin your Lesson: "OUR FATHER IN HEAVEN,"

With knowledge that the Bible commands each disciple to pray regularly and with a desire to pray more consistently in order to secure definite results, I now make the following prayer list.

Pray for These Things:

1. **I'll pray for myself** – for a humble, submissive spirit toward Christ.
2. **For my family** – that I may be a Christian testimony and a blessing to each one of them.
3. **For my pastor** – that God will give him the grace, spiritual power and wisdom to lead, feed, and shepherd the flock.
4. **For my country** – that God will send revival to our nation, especially to those in high positions.
5. **For our missionaries** – for their safety, success, and support. (Write down the missionaries' names and their countries.)

1. _____ country _____
2. _____ country _____
3. _____ country _____

6. **For my lost loved ones and friends.** Write down at least four people whom you will pray for daily.

1. _____ Date prayer answered _____
2. _____ Date prayer answered _____
3. _____ Date prayer answered _____

7. **For evangelists and other special workers**, and call them by name.   James Wilkins

How to Conclude: "IN JESUS' NAME (authority), AMEN."

FOR ADDED BLESSINGS AND GROWTH

"As a man thinketh in his heart so is he" (Proverbs 23:7).

This verse is one of the greatest BIOLOGICAL, PSYCHO-LOGICAL and BIBLICAL PRINCIPLES IN THE WORLD.

WHAT A PERSON THINKS OR WHAT A PERSON IS ON THE INSIDE IS THE TYPE OF PERSON HE REALLY IS AND WILL DICTATE THE TYPE OF LIFE HE WILL MANIFEST ON THE OUTSIDE.

- If one TAKES INTO HIS MIND negative worldly thoughts, then he WILL LIVE A NEGATIVE AND WORLDLY LIFE.

- If one TAKES INTO HIS MIND positive thoughts of faith, then HE WILL LIVE A POSITIVE LIFE OF FAITH.

- One CAN CHANGE A POOR SELF-IMAGE by developing good positive habits.

- One CAN STRENGTHEN ONESELF AND INCREASE FAITH by doing three things:

  1. majoring on good, healthy thoughts,
  2. washing ones mind by reading and memorizing scriptures, and
  3. stating right objectives and positive goals daily.

- ONE CAN DEVELOP A GOOD, HAPPY INNER SELF BY THIS SIMPLE DAILY EXERCISE. (Be sure to check the appropriate block each day.)

A MUST!!   **REPEAT THE DAILY DECLARATIONS AT LEAST EVERY MORNING AND EVENING.**

A MUST!!   **STRIVE TO MEMORIZE THE MEMORY VERSE EACH WEEK.**

DAILY DECLARATION

Repeat Aloud Each Morning And Evening

I will endeavor to keep my eyes and mind upon the Lord, and I will not allow the actions of others to hinder me.

MEMORY VERSE: "If ye then be risen with Christ, seek those things which are above, where Christ sitteth on the right hand of God." (Col. 3:1)

CHECK BLOCK AFTER REPEATING

	Mon	Tues	Wed	Thurs	Fri	Sat	Sun
A.M.							
P.M.							

Is GOD AS
SMART
AS GENERAL MOTORS?

This title may startle you, as it always gets a startled response when I ask a congregation this seemingly dumb question. It seems to catch people off guard. **Is God as smart as General Motors?** There is always one startled Ford owner that makes a quicker recovery than the rest. He answers with a heated **"yes, God is smarter than General Motors!"**

All Car manufacturers know that their latest model with its power, luster, and performance will lose that power, luster, and performance with the wear and tear of time.

Because of this, they print a manual, which lists all the parts for every single model they manufacture. Following the manual, skilled mechanics can restore any car to its original power, performance, and luster.

Is God as smart as General Motors? God, our creator, must have a manual, which, when followed properly, would tune man's life to a level where his life would run smoothly.

If God is as smart as General Motors, **He has a manual**, that when followed will bring any person, male or female, regardless of age or condition, to a place where life is happy and fulfilling.

God's manual is the Holy Bible. At first a person may not understand God's Manual any more than he would a technical part's manual, but if one is serious about being happy and living a successful life, he can find that purpose by reading and following God's manual.

Lesson No. 2

YOU AND THE NEW TESTAMENT FAITH

"One Lord, One Faith, and One Baptism"

INTRODUCTION: Does it really matter what one believes? Is it enough just to be sincere? Is there a proper way to interpret the Bible? Is there a true New Testament faith still in existence today? These questions will be answered in this lesson.

I. THREE WAYS IN WHICH "FAITH" IS USED

There are at least three ways in the New Testament in which the word "faith" is used. They are:

A. Personal Faith unto salvation.

"For by grace are ye saved through faith; and that not of yourselves: [it is] the gift of God; not of works, lest any man should boast" (Ephesians 2:8-9). These verses refer to the personal faith, or trust, the sinner places in Christ when he is saved; i.e., **saving faith**.

B. The trusting Faith of the saved.

"The just (saved) shall live by faith" (Hebrews 10:38). The eleventh chapter of Hebrews is the great faith chapter in the Bible. In this chapter, we have many great achievements for God. They were performed because the individuals believed or had faith in God. God told them to do it. They believed Him and obeyed Him by faith.

C. Faith as "The Faith" or System of Doctrine.

1. *"One Lord, one Faith* (system of religious beliefs), *and one baptism"* (Ephesians 4:5).

2. Webster says that Faith means a system of religious beliefs, creed, denominations, or beliefs.

15

3. When the word "faith" is used in the King James Version, it is used as a system of religious beliefs, and it generally has the definite article "the" in front of it. This rule is without exception in the Greek. When the Bible is referring to "the Faith" as a system of religious beliefs, it always has the definite article "the" in front of it. In this way, one always knows when the word "faith" is being used as a system of religious beliefs.

II   JESUS SAID "MY FAITH"

A.   Jesus had a faith.

1. Jesus told the church at Pergamos, *"You have not denied my faith,"* or literally, you have not denied the system of doctrine (teaching) that is mine (Revelation 2:13).

2. Jesus, after teaching His disciples for three and one-half years, commissioned them by saying, *"Teaching them to observe all things whatsoever I have commanded you:"* (Matthew 28:20). Jesus had an order of things He taught them or "The Faith."

B.   The church in Jerusalem had a faith (Acts 8:1-3).

The Apostle Paul, before his conversion, "made havoc" of the church in Jerusalem (Acts 8:1-3). Years later, he recounted the incident as he wrote to the churches of Galatia. He said, *"Afterwards I came into the regions of Syria and Cilicia; and was unknown by face unto the churches of Judaea which were in Christ: but they had heard only, that he which persecuted us in times past now preacheth the faith which once he destroyed"* (Galatians 1:21-23).

C.   *One will be rewarded for keeping "the faith."*

1. **Statement of fact.** One will not be crowned except he strives lawfully. *"And if a man also strive*

for masteries, [yet] is he not crowned, except he strive lawfully" (II Timothy 2:5). This teaches that God has a proper way of doing things and if we do them the way He commands, we will be crowned or rewarded.

2. **There will be earthly rewards** for keeping the faith. *"For ye are all the children of God by faith in Christ Jesus"* (Galatians 3:26). The word translated "children" is the Greek word "U'ous" which means a full grown son. There are three Greek words translated sons. One means a baby; another means a son of junior or intermediate age; while "U'ous" means a mature or fullgrown son. The definite article is before the word Faith. This verse literally means we are mature sons of God by keeping the faith, or by practicing the proper system of religious beliefs.

3. **This is a tremendous reward.** There are many of God's children who are living a poor, defeated, fearful life. By knowing and practicing the true New Testament faith, a person grows above this. He can be confident, because he knows where he stands with God, what life is all about, where he is going when he dies, and how to serve and please God.

4. **There will be eternal rewards** for keeping the faith. One will be presented HOLY, UNBLAME-ABLE, AND UNREPROVEABLE IN HIS SIGHT if he continues in the faith (Colossians 1:22-23).

    Please note: these are saved, baptized members of the church in Colosse. What a tremendous promise—to be presented to Jesus HOLY, UNBLAMEABLE, AND UNREPROVE-ABLE. You say, "What's the catch?" Yes, there is one, and it is tied up in the little word "IF." One will be presented HOLY, UNBLAMEABLE, and UNREPROVEABLE in His sight, IF, he continues in the faith. It is important what you believe. It is important how you practice what you believe. You will be rewarded for keeping the faith.

5. **Paul rejoiced at his anticipated reward** for keeping "the faith." He said, *"I have fought a good fight, I have finished [my] course* (the job Jesus gave him to do when He saved him), *I have kept the faith:"* (II Timothy 4:7). Then, he almost shouts as he says in **verse 8**, *"Henceforth there is laid up for me a crown of righteousness."* Because Paul fought in the army of God, finished his job, and kept the true teachings of Christ, he was looking forward to HIS REWARD.

III. The "*FAITH that is found in all ages.*

Jesus instituted a system of doctrine. Paul said there was one faith, one Lord, and one baptism. Now we know that there are many faiths or systems of doctrine. Paul meant that there was one true faith. The Bible teaches that there is a true way to interpret every single doctrine in the Bible. The Bible assures the perpetuity of that true New Testament faith.

A. The Faith during the New Testament days.

There had to be a faith during the time of the New Testament. Jesus started it; the church at Jerusalem continued it; and Paul, first persecuted it and then preached it (Acts 8:14; Galatians 1:23).

B. The Faith during the latter days (I Timothy 4:1-3).

1. "Now the Spirit speaketh expressly, that in the LATTER TIMES, some shall depart from the faith giving heed to seducing spirits and doctrines of devils; Speaking lies in hypocrisy; having their conscience seared with a hot iron; forbidding to marry, [and commanding] to abstain from meats.

   a. Notice the time element—*"In the latter times."*

b. *Depart from the faith* (system of doctrine*)
    giving heed to doctrine (teachings) *of devils."*
    What is the doctrine of devils?

    - Forbidding to marry
    - Abstaining from meats
    - The ordinance forbidding priests to marry
      (This ordinance was passed in 1123 AD,
      and is included in this dispensation
      period. Therefore, it is considered *"in the
      latter times.")*

2. **The FAITH** has been in existence from the setting
    up of the church in Acts, through today. This is
    the dispensation period, which is considered as
    the "latter times." It, *"latter times,"* was in effect in
    1123 AD, and some forsook **the Faith**. Some
    could not have departed from the faith in the "latter
    times" if the faith had not continued through that
    time?

C. **The Faith in the last days (II Tomothy 3:1-8).**

1. **In the last days,** men are reprobates concerning
    the faith.

2. **The time is the important element** in proper
    understanding of this passage.   "Last days
    perilous times shall come" (v.1). **Note:** The "last
    days."

3. Paul notes all the conditions, which will prevail
    during the "last days."

4. Then he concludes by saying, *"so do these also
    resist the truth: men of corrupt minds, reprobate
    concerning the faith."* How could these be
    reprobates toward "the faith" during the "last days"
    unless the "faith" existed?

D. **"The Faith" found in all ages restated.**

1. **Jesus started it**—the church at Jerusalem, and the Apostle Paul continued it by preaching the gospel through the remainder of the New Testament days.

2. **Some left "the faith"** during the "latter times."

3. **Some were reprobates** toward it in the "last days."

4. **Jesus assured the church** he would be with them throughout the church age if they taught what he commanded them to teach. *"Teaching them to observe all things whatsoever I have commanded you: and, lo, I am with you always, [even] unto the end of the world"* (age).

5. **The Bible teaches** that Jesus established a true New Testament faith during his ministry and that that true faith has continued down through the ages, and it is still being taught today.

IV. THE BIBLE ADMONISHES ONE TO BE ESTABLISHED IN THE FAITH

A. *"As ye therefore received Christ Jesus the Lord, so walk ye in Him; rooted and built up in Him and ESTABLISHED IN THE FAITH. AS YE HAVE BEEN TAUGHT"* (Colossians 2:6-7).

B *"...that ye stand fast in one spirit, with one mind striving together for the faith of the gospel;"* (Philippians 1:27b).

C. *"...it was needful for me to write unto you, and exhort [you] that ye should earnestly contend for the faith which was once delivered unto the saints"* (Jude 3b).

These scriptures are presented so clearly by the Holy Spirit that they need no further comment. The fact that Jesus had a faith that has been perpetuated by the Holy Spirit, and that a person would be rewarded if he continues in the faith, has been proven. If this is so, then this should be enough to cause one to want to be established in the faith.

V. **THE FAITH IS TO BE PRACTICED AS WELL AS BELIEVED.** The emphasis in the New Testament is on doing as well as believing.

A. **Jesus and the New Testament faith.**

1, **Dr. Luke reminds Theophilus** that Jesus began to do and to teach (Acts 1:1). **Notice:** The **doing** comes before the **teaching**.

2. **Jesus, referring to the scribes and Pharisees** said, *"This people draweth nigh unto me with their mouth, and honoureth me with [their] lips; but their heart is far from me"* (Matthew 15:8). Jesus said, *"but do not ye after their works: for they say, and do not"* (Matthew 23:3), and he strongly denounced the scribes and Pharisees as hypocrites.

B. **Paul "Did" versus Paul "Said."**

1. **Paul said.** The Holy Spirit used the Apostle Paul to write fourteen (14) books of the New Testament. In proving all the major New Testament doctrines, Paul is quoted very often. This is good! This is what a Bible student ought to do. He should have a *"Thus saith the Lord,"* or a **chapter and verse** for everything he believes. It is GOOD TO SAY—Paul said!

2. **Paul did.** PLEASE NOTICE what **Paul did** as well as what **Paul said.**

a. He went night and day with tears (Acts 20:31).

b.   He went from house to house (Acts 20:20).

c.   He became all things to all men that he may save some (1 Corinthians 9:22).

d.   He kept back nothing that was profitable (Acts 20:19-20); "But gave his all (Romans 1:14-15).

e.   He fasted (II Corinthians 11:27).

f.   He suffered more than almost any man (II Corinthians 11:23-28).

g.   He finally gave his life as a martyr (II Timothy 4:6-8).

C. **Jesus never intended for people to stress the letter of the law and call it "standing for the faith."**

1.   **He said,** *"Worship God in spirit and in truth"* (John 4:23).

2.   **He said,** *"By this shall all men know you are my disciples* (true disciples) *THAT YOU LOVE ONE ANOTHER"* (John 13:35). You don't cut them down because they have a slight doctrinal difference. You can't convert and teach people by beating them over the head, or by having a self-righteous, holier than thou attitude.

3.   **Contending for the faith** means being strong in the Bible and sweet in the Spirit.

4.   **In closing,** one question remains to be asked, *"Examine yourselves, whether you be in the faith?"* (II Corinthians 13:5)

MY FAITH

Monday (Three Ways)

1. Personal faith or _____ Faith is the first mentioned in this lesson.

2. Who are "the just" referred to in Hebrews 10:38? _____
    _____

3. Where is the faith chapter found in the Bible? _____
    _____

4. Webster defines "The Faith" as ___ _____ _____
    _____ _____

5. How do you know when faith means the Faith as a system of religious belief? ___ _____ _____ _____
    _____ _____ ___ _____ ____ ___

Tuesday
(Jesus said, "My Faith")

1. What Church did not deny the true faith? _____

2. Jesus taught the disciples for _____ years.

3. We grow into mature sons of God by keeping _____
    _____ (Galatians 3:26).

4. We will be presented Holy, unblameable, and unreproveable if we continue in the _____
    Colossians 1:21-23.

5. Paul was expecting to be rewarded for fighting a _____
    fight, for _____ the course, and for keeping the
    _____.

Wednesday
(The Faith Found in all Ages)

1. Who started the true faith? _____

2. Who first persecuted it then preached it? _____

3. The Spirit speaketh expressly in the _____ times.

4. Men will be reprobates toward the faith during the

   _____ _____.

5. Jesus says, *"Lo, I will be with you always, even until the end of the world"* or _____.

Thursday
(The Bible Admonishes)

1. How did the disciples in Colosse learn the faith?
   Colossians 2:7-8. They were _____.

2. Stand fast in _____ Spirit, with one mind, striving for
   _____ _____ of the Gospel (Philippians 1:27).

3. Jude said earnestly contend for the _____(Jude 3).

4. The faith has been perpetuated by the _____

   _____.

5. Since the Bible Commands it, one should want to be
   _____ in the faith.

Friday
(Paul Did Verses Paul Said)

1. Jesus began _____ _____ and then _____ _____ (Acts1:1).
2. Why did Jesus denounce the Pharisees? They say _____ _____ _____.
3. Paul went night and _____ with _____.
4. Paul went from house ___ _____. (Acts 20:20).
5. He became _____ _____ to all men that he could save some. (I Corinthians 9:22).

Having studied this lesson and found that Jesus established a true faith and assured its perpetuity throughout all ages, I now promise the Lord that I will first submit myself to Him and to pastor _____, whom God gave to help me learn. By God's grace, I will be true to the Lord, His Faith, and His cause until He comes.

_____   _____
Name   Date

Questions to ask the discipler:

DAILY DECLARATION

Repeat Aloud Each Morning And Evening

I will strive to contend for the faith by being strong in the Bible and sweet in the Spirit.

MEMORY VERSE: *"By this shall all men know that ye are my disciples, if ye have love one to another"* (John 13:35).

CHECK BLOCK AFTER REPEATING

	Mon	Tues	Wed	Thurs	Fri	Sat	Sun
A.M.							
P.M.							

"OVERHEARD IN THE ORCHARD"

Said the Robin to the Sparrow
"I should really like to know
Why the anxious human beings
Rush around and worry so?"

Said the Sparrow to the Robin
"Friend, I think that it must be
that they have no heavenly faither
such as cares for you and me."

Elizabeth Cheney

Lesson no. 3

GOD'S INSPIRED WORD

II Timothy 3:16-17

INTRODUCTION: The Bible is a divinely inspired library of 66 books (39 in the Old Testament and 27 in the New Testament) written by forty different writers over a period of about 1500 years. The word "Bible" comes from the Greek word "biblia," which means "Books." "The Books" was the name of this library of 66 books until shortly after A.D.400 when it received the name "Bible."

I.   HOW DID WE RECEIVE THE BIBLE?

A.   Men of God were inspired by the Holy Spirit.

1.   **All scripture is given by inspiration of God** (II Timothy. 3:16.)

2.   **Inspiration, comes from the compound Greek word:** Theos, God, and Pneustos, Breathed. All scripture is "God breathed."

3.   **Peter stated,** *"But Holy men of God spake as they were moved by the Holy Spirit"* (II Peter 1:21).

      The Greek verb is translated "Moved," in II Peter 1:21. "Being moved" means literally, to be moved upon, or to be carried along; i.e., as by a strong current or mighty influence. The verb form is the passive participle, and can be translated. "when moved upon or borne along by...." This distinctly teaches that the Scriptures were not written by mere men, or at their suggestion, but by men moved upon, prompted, yea, indeed, driven by the promptings of the Holy Spirit.

28

4. **Jeremiah is a perfect illustration** of God moving upon or breathing upon men to write the Word of God. After severe persecution, He decided he would not prophesy any more, but after God breathed in his soul, he stated, "But His Word was in my heart like a burning fire, shut up in my bones, and I could not stay [refrain]." (Jeremiah 20:9)

B. **These inspired men wrote on goat skins, sheep skins and papyrus scrolls.**

1. God used about forty different writers.

2. They lived as much as 1500 years apart in time.

3. They came from different backgrounds.

    But all of them were "moved upon by the Holy Spirit and directed to write where they were in perfect harmony with each other. The Holy Spirit, the author of the Bible, superintended each writer.

C. **These men wrote in three different languages.**

1. **Hebrew:** Most of the Old Testament was written in Hebrew.

2. **Chaldee or Aramaic:** Parts of Daniel, Ezra and Jeremiah were written in Chaldee.

3. **Greek:** The New Testament was written in Koine Greek.

4. **Hebrew and Greek** are now dead or un-changing languages. The meaning of original words have not changed since they were written. This means that men can study the original languages and receive the same truth and knowledge as when they were written.

5. **There are hundreds** of other languages and dialects in addition to our English language. The

King James Version (1611 AD) is the word of God, and the only acceptable translation to this author, and the only one he has ever recommended.

D. **For hundreds of years, these Books were copied by hand.**

1. **The scribes who copied** these books were the most highly educated and the skilled men of their day.

2. **One objection to the Bible**, by its critics, is it was hand copied and there are so many mistakes. People who are, knowingly or unknowingly, ignorant make this criticism. Some times a copyist might make a mistake. He may use "the" instead of "a" or "that." He may use the singular form of the word instead of the plural form. But when you have 1500 to 2000 manuscripts of that part of the Bible, each one copied by hand, and many centuries old, and only 10 or 20 with that simple mistake in it, then the mistake is easily recognized and corrected.

3. **We do not have to depend on the reliability of the translators** nor the truthfulness of men, because God has promised to preserve His Word. **Jesus stated:**

"Heaven and earth shall pass away, but my words shall not pass away" (Matthew 24:35).

"For verily I say unto you, Till heaven and earth pass, one jot or one tittle shall in no wise pass from the law, till all be fulfilled" (Matthew 5:18).

Jesus had previously told the apostles that the old testament scriptures were inspired. **David** was inspired to proclaim,

"For ever, O LORD, thy word is settled in heaven" (Psalms 119:86).

II. INTERNAL PROOFS THAT THE BIBLE IS GOD'S ETERNAL, INSPIRED WORD

A. The claims of the writers of the Bible.

1. **Paul**—*"All scripture is given by inspiration of God"* (II Timothy 3:16).

2. **Peter**—*"Holy men of God spake [as they were] moved by the Holy Ghost"* (II Peter 1:21).

There are 263 direct quotations in the New Testament from the Old Testament, and there are approximately 350 indirect allusions to the Old Testament.

The expression, **"thus saith the Lord"** occurs over 2,000 times.

B. The Old Testament, as it is today, was upon earth during Jesus' personal ministry.

1. **Jesus not only set His approval upon it**, but divided it into three divisions: *"...which were written in the Law of Moses, and in the prophets, and in the Psalms."* (Luke 24:44)

C. Jesus PRE-AUTHENTICATED the New Testament in John 16.

1. **Jesus set His approval upon the Old Testament during His personal ministry**. In the last service with His disciples, the night before he was crucified, he told them about the further writings which would be given by the Holy Spirit, which would complete the Holy Canon. None of the New Testament books had been written during His ministry. One of the requirements to write was that an apostle was to have accompanied with Jesus from the time of John the Baptist, until Jesus was caught up to heaven (Acts 1:21-22). They had heard every lesson, seen every miracle and had been

personally discipled by Jesus. Events had to happen and experiences must have been lived through before the apostles were equipped to become part of the elite group which the Holy Spirit used as human tools in writing God's eternal word. In **V.12**, Jesus said,

"I have yet many things to say unto you, but ye cannot bear them now."

In **V. 25,** Jesus told them,

"These things have I spoken unto you in proverbs: but the time cometh, when I shall no more speak unto you in proverbs, **but I shall shew you plainly of the Father.***"*

He then explained that the teaching he would give would come from Him through the Holy Spirit. His exact explanation concerning this future teaching and guidance of the Holy Spirit is recorded in John 16:13. He said,

"Howbeit when he, the Spirit of truth, is come, he will guide you into all truth: for he shall not speak of himself; but whatsoever he shall hear, [that] shall he speak:..."

This is the same procedure that he had Moses and the others use to write the inspired Old Testament books. He concludes the verse by saying, *"...and he will shew you things to come."*

These experiences were necessary so that the Holy Spirit could draw to their attention the teachings and actions of Jesus as the Spirit superintended them in writing the New Testament books and epistles. Jesus had trained and then qualified the apostles to be used as instruments of the Holy Spirit as a major part in completing His eternal perfect word. The apostle Paul was later called and inspired by the

Holy Spirit to contribute his part in the holy
writings.

2. **Jesus was speaking directly to the apostles**.
    The final church services, which Jesus
    conducted as the pastor of the church, are
    recorded in chapters 13 through 16 of John. It is
    in the latter part of the services, recorded in
    chapter 16, that Jesus informed the disciples
    about the necessity of His death and the ministry
    of the comforter (Holy Spirit).

3. **An illustration of the preservation of God's
    word**. During a dark period in early American
    history, there were more books entitled, "The
    age of Reason" written by the Leading atheist,
    Thomas Payne, than there were Holy Bibles.
    Mr. Payne boasted that he would rid the world of
    Bibles through the assault and presentation of
    his views of atheism.   God sent revival to
    America. Thomas Payne's book has long been
    discarded, and the very printing press, which he
    used to attack the Bible, was later used to print
    millions and millions of Bibles.   God has
    miraculously preserved His word through many
    such dark days.

D. **The Bible is Under Attack.**

In 1960, when most of this book was written as a
thesis, the average person in the United States
believed the Bible to be the word of God, and
respected it as such. The King James Version (1611)
was reverenced and accepted as the perfect, inspired
word of God. Under the guise of making it easier to
read, there have been many new translations of the
Bible.   All attempts have fallen far short of their
publicized goals. In fact, several are perversions of
the Bible; instead of clarifying the Bible, the very
opposite has happened. They have undermined the
Bible and caused great confusion and harm.

33

E. The Bible was written with the masses in mind, so that the common man can understand it.

In order to understand the Bible, one must be born again, have someone teach him his spiritual phonics, and then prayerfully study the Bible in order to learn how to read and comprehend its eternal truths. The Bible was written with the masses in mind, and the common man can comprehend its teachings.

F. God never intended that the bible be read like a novel.

The Bible is God's manual for the Human race. Man is to be directed by it in order for him to understand His purpose in the light of eternity. God has commanded man to diligently study it. He has promised temporal and eternal blessings to those who search the Scriptures as men who search for hidden treasures. (Proverbs 2:3-5) A casual reader will never receive much good from reading the Bible.

III. SOME WONDERFUL WORDS ABOUT THE WONDERFUL WORD

A. The Bible Is

The Bible is a light for our understanding
The Bible is a mirror for our self-knowledge
The Bible is a sword for our conflict
The Bible is honey for our delight
The Bible is a hammer for our obstinacy
The Bible is milk for our nourishment
The Bible is meat for our strengthening
The Bible is a seed for our sowing
The Bible is gold for our enrichment

B. The Bible is Forever

Communists may try to suppress it. Atheists will deny it, scoff at it, and ridicule it. Professors will try to discredit it, and vicious attacks have been made on it and against it.

Enemies have sought to destroy it. New versions and perversions seek to do away with it, but still the blessed Old Book is Forever.

The Bible—being inspired is infallible
        being inspired is dependable
        being inspired is eternal
        being inspired is indestructible

"Despised and torn in pieces
By infidels decried
The thunderbolts of hatred
The haughty cynics pride

All these have railed against it
In this or other lands
Yet dynasties have fallen
And still the Bible stands."
        James M. Gray

C. Jesus Christ is the Supreme Wonder of the Bible

The Old Testament conceals Christ
    The New Testament reveals Christ
The Old Testament enfolds Christ
    The New Testament unfolds Christ
The Old Testament promises Christ
    The New Testament presents Christ
The Old Testament pictures Christ
    The New Testament produces Christ
The Old Testament symbolizes Christ
    The New Testament sacrifices Christ
The Old Testament prophesies Christ
    The New Testament proclaims Christ
The Old Testament is law, which Christ fulfilled
    The New Testament is love, which Christ exhibits
The secret of the unity of the Bible is Jesus
The secret of the strength of the Bible is Jesus
The secret of the beauty of the Bible is Jesus
    He is the Alpha—and the Omega

He is the first and the last
Take away the Bible and you take away Christ
Take away Christ and you take away the found-
ation of our lives.

Note: Some wonderful words about the wonderful
Word. (Many of the quotes in this section are from
Dr. Earl K. Oldham's book, So It's A Miracle.)

D. The Bible is our Manual

When Paul stated that the Bible would thoroughly furnish the believers in all good works, he is simply
stating that the Bible was placed on this earth to
serve as the manual for the human race. God made
us! He gives man his life and maintains it, so it is only
logical that he would place a manual or an instruction
book upon this earth to direct it. By following the
manual, he can live a happy and fruitful life. **One
must learn how to read the manual** if he is follow it
successfully and fulfill his purpose while on this earth.

IV. EXTERNAL PROOF THAT THE BIBLE IS GOD'S ETERNAL, INSPIRED WORD

A. The preservation of the Bible

The fact that the Bible is enjoying its greatest
circulation today is evidence that it is inspired. In
spite of all the persecution, bannings, burnings, and
criticisms, the Divine Book is being read by more
people today than ever before. This is an illustration
of the preservation of God's Word.

B. The unity of the Book

Although it was written during a period of 1500
years by about 40 different writers who had varied
backgrounds, there are no contradictions in the Bible.
Can you imagine the change and contradictions,
which any science book would have, if you took

the thesis on its subject from over a period of 1500 years.

Think about the development in the field of medical science over the last 1500 years or in the computer field in the last 15 years. The only explanation for the harmony found in a book where 40 writers, who lived over a vast period of 1500 years, is that they were the human tools God used to bring His eternal book into existence.

C. Fulfilled prophecy proves the Bible to be inspired

To accurate foretelling of future events, proves the inspiration of the Bible. Left to ourselves, we cannot know what will happen tomorrow, but the Bible prophesied events hundreds of years before they came to pass. Some of the prophecies had to do with the fall of Babylon, the scattering and the preservation of the Jewish nation, the birth and death of Jesus, the rise and fall of the Roman Empire, and numerous other events. These events were prophesied hundreds of years before they came to pass. The Bible is the only book that has been 100% accurate in all its predictions.

D. The superior, lofty concept of the Bible proves it to be inspired

When the philosophy of the world is dog eat dog; might is right; and do others before they do you; the Bible teaches us to love our neighbor; feed our enemy; and help our fellow man. Its teachings concerning marriage, the home, and raising children; when followed, lifts a nation up, and its society is one of lawfulness, peace, and prosperity.

E. Harmony with proven science proves the Bible to be inspired

When rightly interpreted, the Bible harmonizes with all known facts concerning the physical make up of the universe, the constitution of man, his complex nature and being, the order of animal and plant life, and all other true facts of science.

Much harm has been caused in recent years by Christians trying to harmonize the Bible with some theory of science. They blindly accept all claims of science as true and try to fit the Bible into that theory. This is not necessary, because the Bible is completely true and all true science is in perfect agreement with the Bible.

F. **The transforming effect of the Bible on people's lives proves it to be a Supernatural Book**

When one considers the dramatic change upon the character and conduct of people who read and obey the teachings of the Bible, one has to realize that the Bible is inspired.

Biblical Examples of Changed Lives. Notice the change in Saul to Paul; the 3,000 skeptics on the day of Pentecost were changed to 3,000 disciples; drunkards became sober, God fearing men; harlots became righteous, spirit-filled women; etc.

Perhaps the most vivid example of change, which the Bible produces in the life of an individual, is the example of the Apostle Paul. Before his conversion to Christianity, he hated and persecuted Christians. He led expeditions to destroy the church and had many of its members jailed or executed. *"He made havoc of the Church"* (Acts 8:3). This harsh Saul (Saul means defiant) was converted and became Paul (means humility). He literally became the leading person demonstrating God's love toward sinful man. He suffered trials, beatings, and indescribable hardships as he gave his life to preach the Gospel, represent God, and win and disciple people.

A Broad Biblical Scale. On a broader scale, there were 3,000 hard core members of the Jewish faith, which came to Jerusalem to worship God on the day of Pentecost and returned to their homelands as Christian missionaries. Why the total change? It was because of the influence of the Living Word and their growth in the written word.

A Personal Scale. There were many things which were paramount in changing the author's life; a travelling salesman selling family Bibles found a 16 year old lost kid with some money, and he sold me my first Bible, and later, God saving me when I cried out to Him in desperation. I rejoice every day, **because He changed my life forever**. However, the primary thing, which changed my life then, and has affected me most since then, was when I learn how to read and study the Bible.

What good is a Bible if the person doesn't read it? For all intent and purposes to many people, the Bible is just another book. However, if someone teaches a new convert how to rightly divide the word so he can understand it, right after he is saved, then the chances are good that he will enjoy reading the Bible and grow into maturity.

The perfect word of God has exerted the greatest influence on my life, and I am a living testimony of its transforming influence.

There are thousands of examples of alcoholics made sober, and wicked, depraved sinners converted to loving ministering saints. When a person considers this powerful effect the Bible has upon people who read and then follow its teaching, he must conclude it is because of **THE SUPERNATURAL BOOK**.

COMMENTS FROM GREAT MEN OF THE PAST

The following are a few comments of great men concerning their view of the Bible.

Abraham Lincoln: "I believe the Bible is the best gift God has ever given to man. All the good from the Saviour of the world is communicated to us through this book."

W. E. Gladstone: "I have known ninety-five of the world's great men in my time, and of these, eighty-seven were followers of the Bible. The Bible is stamped with a Specialty of Origin, and an immeasurable distance separates it from all competitors."

George Washington: "It is impossible to rightly govern the world without God and the Bible."

Napoleon: "The Bible is no mere book, but a Living Creature, with a power that conquers all that oppose it."

Queen Victoria: "That book accounts for the supremacy of England."

Daniel Webster: "If there is anything in my thoughts or style to commend, the credit is due to my parents for instilling in me an early love of the Scriptures. If we abide by the principles taught in the Bible, our country will go on prospering and to prosper; but if we and our posterity neglect its instructions and authority, no man can tell how sudden a catastrophe may overwhelm us and bury all our glory in profound obscurity."

Thomas Huxley: "The Bible is the sheet-anchor of our liberties.".

Horace Greeley: "It is impossible to enslave mentally or socially Bible reading people. The principles of the Bible are the groundwork of human freedom."

Andrew Jackson: "That book, sir, is the rock on which our republic rests."

HOW DID WE RECEIVE

Monday

(Introduction)

1. The Bible is a library of _____ books, written by about _____ writers over a period of about _____ years.

2. The word "Bible" comes from the Greek word, _____, which means _____ _____.

3. Men of God were inspired by the _____ _____.

4. Inspiration comes from the compound Greek word _____, which means God and _____, which means _____ _____.

5. The men wrote in three languages, _____, Chaldee or Aramaic, and _____ _____.

Tuesday

(Section D and Internal Proofs)

1. If there are 1,500 to 2,000 manuscripts and only 15 or 20 have a simple mistake; the mistake is _____ _____ and corrected.

2. We do not have to depend on the _____ of the translators.

3. God has promised to preserve His _____. (Matt. 5:18; 24:35)

4. There are _____ direct quotations in the New Testament taken from the Old Testament.

5. Jesus not only set His approval upon the Old _____ in Luke 24:44-45, but He _____ it into three _____.

   a. _____ b. _____ c. _____

Wednesday
(Wonderful Words)

1. The Bible is a _____ for our understanding.
2. The Bible being inspired is _____.
3. The Old Testament conceals Christ–the New Testament _____ Christ.
4. The secret of the Unity of the Bible is _____.
5. The secret of the _____ of the Bible is Jesus.

Thursday
(External Proofs)

1. The _____, _____ _____ of the Bible proves it is inspired.
2. The unity of the Bible proves it is _____.
3. Fulfilled prophecy proves ____ _____ to be inspired.
4. Harmony with proven _____ proves the Bible to be _____.
5. The transforming effects of the _____ on people's lives, proves it to be a supernatural _____.

Friday
(About the Bible)

1. George Washington said, "It is impossible to rightly govern the _____ without God and the _____.

2. Abraham Lincoln had this to say, "I believe the _____ is the best gift God has ever given to _____.

3. "The _____ is no mere book, but a living creature, with a power that _____ all that oppose it." Napoleon.

4. "The Bible is worth all other books which have ever been _____." Patrick Henry.

5. Andrew Jackson stated, "That Book, Sir, is the _____ on which our republic rests."

Having studied this lesson on God's inspired Word, I am convinced that the Bible is God's infallible, eternal Word. I will study it each day, abide by its direction, and conform to its teaching. I will endeavor to learn it well enough to teach others also. I Peter 3:15.

_____ _____
Name   **Date**

Questions to ask the discipler.

DAILY DECLARATION

Repeat Aloud Each Morning And Evening

"The Bible is worth all other books which have ever been printed." Patrick Henry

MEMORY VERSE: *"All Scripture is given by inspiration of God, and is profitable for doctrine, for reproof, for correction, for instruction in righteousness: That the man of God may be perfect, thoroughly furnished unto all good works."* (II Timothy 3:16-17)

CHECK BLOCK AFTER REPEATING

	Mon	Tues	Wed	Thurs	Fri	Sat	Sun
A.M.							
P.M.							

SEVEN LOGICAL PRINCIPLES OF LIFE

I.   There is a God OR there is no God.

II. If there is a God, THEN God made man.[a]

III. If God made man, THEN He did so for a purpose.[b]

IV. If God made man, THEN there MUST BE A BOOK, **which reveals that purpose** to man.[c]

V.   If God **made man for a purpose**, THEN there must be a FUTURE DAY in which man will stand before his Creator and GIVE ACCOUNT of **how he fulfilled his purpose.**[d]

VI. If God made man for a purpose, **then** man will be rewarded or penalized in direct proportion as to HOW HE FULFILLED **that purpose.**[e]

VII. **If all of the above is true**, and God gives you life and continuance on this earth, THEN **He has a rightful claim to your love and obedience.**[f]

WHAT IS YOUR PURPOSE ON THIS EARTH?

a.	Genesis 1:1	d.	John 5:28-29
b.	Genesis 1:26-27	e.	Ecclesiastes
c.	II Timothy 3:16-17	f.	I Corinthians 6:19-20

RIGHT DIVISION OF THE BIBLE

II Timothy 2:15

"Study to show thyself approved UNTO GOD, A WORKMAN that needeth not be ashamed, RIGHTLY DIVIDING the Word of Truth." (II Timothy 2:15).

INTRODUCTION: Perhaps there is no other realm in religious circles where there is a more obvious weakness than in the realm of rightly dividing the word of truth. The proof of this statement is manifested in the many contradictory beliefs stemming from the same scriptures. There is a real need for people to learn to rightly divide the Bible.

I. THE RIGHT DIVISION IS MADE BY STUDY

A. There is a RIGHT way

1. This forceful command to study in order to rightly divide the Bible, proves there is a right way to view every doctrine in God's Word.

2. Seek the help of the Author. One of the many works of the Holy Spirit is to aid the believer in understanding the Bible. The Holy Spirit is the author of the Bible, and one should pray earnestly for His guidance as he studies God's Word.

3. One must realize that many times wicked men or even the Devil may be speaking, so one should prayerfully seek God's leadership as he studies.

II. THE GRAND (large) DIVISION OF THE BIBLE

A. There are two natural divisions of the Bible

1. The natural division in the Bible is obvious. There is the Old Testament and the New Testament.

2. The Word "Testament" means covenant or agreement.

A. The Old Testament has three divisions.
(Luke 24:44-45):

1. **The Law of Moses.** Most scholars agree that this division is made up of the first 17 books of the Bible: Genesis through Esther.

2. **The Prophets** This dividion includes all of the books from Isaiah through the remainder of the Old Testament: seventeen books in all.

3. **Psalms** This third division includes 5 books: Job, Psalms, Proverbs, Ecclesiastes, and The Song of Solomon.

B. The New Testament has three logical parts.

1. **Historical books** The books which are primarily historical are: Matthew, Mark, Luke, John, and the Book of Acts.

2. **Doctrinal books** There are twenty-one epistles or letters, which make up this section, which are basically doctrinal. If you include the Book of Hebrews, fourteen of these letters were written by Paul.

3. **A prophetic book** The Book of Revelation is the book in the New Testament which is primarily prophetic.

III. THERE MUST BE RIGHT DIVISION FOR PROPER UNDERSTANDING OF THE WORD

A. All of the Old Testament is inspired.

1. **In this section** we are not discussing inspiration of the Word, but we are considering rightly dividing the Word. All of the Bible, the entire 66 books, is the inspired Word of God.

2. **In consideration of rightly dividing the Word**, there is one expression which must be clearly understood, and that expression is, "Rule of faith and practice."

   a. Rule means standard or what we go by.

   b. Faith means "the faith" or what we believe. People always ask, "What faith are you?" We understand this to mean what denominational persuasion or church doctrine do you believe in?

   c. By practice, we mean how to practice or do the things we believe.

3. **By rule of faith and practice,** we mean what we believe or go by, and how we practice or observe it.

4. **The reason** Jesus divided the Old Testament into three parts is because we are not under all three divisions today as our rule of faith and practice.

B The Law was done away when fulfilled by Jesus

1. Jesus said that we were under all of the law or none of the law as our rule of faith and practice. Jesus said, in Matthew 5:17-18, *"Think not that I am come to destroy the law or the prophets* (two of the three parts of the Old Testament); *I am not come to destroy, but to fulfill!"* Why did he

come? He did not come to destroy the law or the prophets but to fulfill them. Then he went on to state, *"For verily I say unto you, till heaven and earth pass, one jot* (like a dot over the English letter 'i') *or one tittle* (like a crossing of the English letter 't') *shall in no way pass from the law, till all be fulfilled."* Jesus emphatically states that the smallest part of the Mosaic Law would stay in effect until all of it was fulfilled. All of the minor parts of the Mosaic Law and all of the ceremonial part of the law is still in effect today (as our rule of faith or practice) or none of them are.

2. The TEN COMMANDMENTS were written by God in stone.

   The only record of God's writing that we have is the Ten Commandments. God wrote the Ten Commandments in stone and gave them to Moses on Mt. Sinai.

   a. In II Corinthians 3:7-11, Paul refers to that which was written in stone (clearly the Ten Commandments) as the ministration of death. In the same passage he refers to that which was written and engraved in stone (the Ten Commandments) as the ministration of condemnation and said it was **Done Away**. In order to pinpoint that he was referring to the Ten Commandments, he tells of the brightness of Moses' face when he came down from Mt. Sinai, after seeing the backside of God. This reference to Moses' face makes it absolutely positive that Paul was referring to the Ten Commandments as the ministration of death and condemnation, and that they were done away with as our rule of faith and practice.

   b. In Colossians 2:14-17, Paul said that Jesus fulfilled all the demands of the Mosaic Law and took it out of the way as our rule of faith and practice by nailing it to His Cross. Since Jesus fulfilled all of the types, symbols, and requirements of the Law, it was taken out of the way as the rule of faith and practice.

C. The division referred to as "the Prophets" was done away as our rule of faith and practice.

1.   Jesus referred to the division of the prophets along with the division of the law in Luke 16:16 and stated that these two divisions of the Old Testament were in effect until John (John the Baptist [the last O.T. prophet and the first N. T. preacher]), but since that time (the time of John) the Kingdom of God has been preached, and all men pressed into it. This simply means that there was a change in dispensation (method of God's dealing with mankind) or age (time period in which God dealt in that method with mankind).

2.   Under the Law, the Jews were required to bring an animal to be sacrificed, which testified of their faith in the atoning work of the coming Messiah (Jesus). After Jesus came, which fulfilled the types and rewarded their faith, there was no longer any need for them to offer a lamb because the real Lamb of God had come.

3.   In Hebrews 1:1-2, it tells us that in times past, or in previous dispensations, God spoke to the fathers (previous believers) through the prophets *"but hath in the last days"* (present dispensation) spoken unto us by His Son. Therefore, we can see in these two scriptures that there has been a change in dispensations (the way God deals with mankind). We are living in this new age or present dispensation.

D. We are commanded to use the division of the Psalms today.

1. **Paul told the Ephesian church**, *"Speaking to yourselves in Psalms."* (Ephesians 5:19).

2. **The Colossians were admonished**, *"Let the word of Christ dwell in you richly, and all wisdom; teaching and admonishing one another in psalms."* (Colossians 3:16; 1 Corinthians 14:26).

3. **In the division of Psalms, there are five books.** People of all ages need the message, which is contained in these five books. Ecclesiastes 3:14 states that what God does, He does perfectly. Since God, the Holy Spirit, is the author of the five books, they are perfect and do not need to be repeated again in the New Testament. Therefore, God divided the Old Testament into three parts and fulfilled two of the three divisions and incorporated the third into the new faith and practice, which are the Psalms and the New Testament. When one realizes the central message of each of these books, he will realize that all believers (in all ages) had/have need of these books.

    a. **The Book of Job** – Job answers the question of why a righteous man suffers. It shows that the righteous man, through God's grace, will overcome and triumph.

    b. **The Book of Psalms** – This book teaches us to say "A-men!" and to praise the Lord! To have complete trust and faith in the Lord through our earthly journey and to praise Him as we travel toward Heaven.

    c. **The Book of Proverbs** – This is the book by which a father is to raise his children. What a tremendous need there is in the world today for the Book of Proverbs, God's book, to be read and followed so as to raise our children up in the way they should go.

d.   **The Book of Ecclesiastes** – Many people are asking, "Who am I? What is this life all about?" The Book of Ecclesiastes answers these questions. It clearly tells us what life is all about and how to live and be happy.

e.   **The Book of the Song of Solomon** – This book shows the love between the Bride and the Bridegroom. It illustrates the love and the attitude that the church should have toward Christ and His Second Coming.

E.   The Law and the Prophets still hold an important place in our churches today.

1.   **The foundation of the Bible** rests upon the Law and the Prophets. They tell us where we came from and who we are. They furnish most of the prophecies, which were fulfilled in the New Testament. Without the Law and Prophets, the rest of the Bible would not make good sense.

2.   **The Divisions of the Law and the Prophets** are used for history, types, prophecy and admonitions today.

3.   **These two divisions** are just as important as ever, and they are just as inspired as ever. However, in order to properly divide the Word of God, one must understand that two of these three divisions in the Old Testament were fulfilled (the Law and the Prophets) and taken out of the way as our rule of faith and practice for today. The New Testament superseded them. All of the moral teachings, which are eternal, were reincorporated in the New Testament. Psalms and the New Testament make up the perfect infallible rule of faith and practice which the churches and Christians are under today.

4.   **We use the King James Version (1611 AD).** There is no easy way of learning the Bible. One must seek the leadership of the Holy Spirit and

apply himself to the study of the Word if he is to grow into a mature Christian. The King James Version is the Word of God, so study it carefully. Do not fall into the snare of turning to a version or translation because it is easier to understand. Nothing great has ever been accomplished through taking the path of least resistance. You can understand the Bible if you apply yourself to a prayerful, deliberate study. Jesus commanded, *"search the scriptures"* (John 5:39).

MONDAY

(Introduction)

1. How can we escape being ashamed when we stand before God? (II Timothy 2:15); *"Rightly* _____ _____ _____ _____ _____."

2. Who should a child of God try to be approved by: man, God, or denomination? By _____.

3. Where is the most obvious weakness in religious circles today? Of _____ _____ the Word of _____.

4. What proof do we have for that statement? In the many _____ _____ stemming from _____ _____ _____.

5. There is a need to learn to _____ _____ the _____ _____ _____.

TUESDAY

(Right Division by Study)

1. The forceful command to study proves what? _____ _____ ____ _____ _____ _____ _____ _____ _____ _____ _____ _____.

2. One should pray earnestly for the _____ _____ guidance as he studies the Bible.

3. How is right division of the Bible made? _____&_____.

4. Wicked men and even _____ _____ are quoted in the Bible.

5. Because of this, one must _____ _____ the leadership of God as he studies.

54

WEDNESDAY

(Grand Division of the Bible)

1. What is the grand division of the Bible? The _____ and _____ Testaments.

2. Testament means _____ or _____.

3. There are _____ parts in the Old Testament.

4. What are they? (1) _____ of _____, (2) _____ and (3) _____.

5. What are the three logical parts of the New Testament? (1) _____ books, (2) _____ and (3) a _____ book.

THURSDAY

(Right Division—Proper Understanding)

1. In this section we are studying _____ _____ not inspiration.

2. How many books of the Bible are inspired? _____ _____

3. What does "rule" mean? _____ _____ _____ _____ _____ _____.

4. What does "faith" mean? _____ ___ _____ _____.

5. What do we mean by "practice"? _____ _____ _____ _____ _____ _____ _____.

FRIDAY

(The Law, Prophets, and Psalms or Section III B, C, and D)

1. The Ten Commandments were written by God _____ _____.

2. The law and prophets were until _____.

3. What book did God give which aids fathers in raising children? The _____ of _____.

4. What two divisions of the Old Testament were fulfilled as the rule of faith and practice? _____ and _____.

5. What are we under today as our rule of faith and practice? The _____ _____ and _____.

Having studied this lesson and learned that there is a proper method to divide the Word of God, I will prayerfully study the Bible in order to show myself approved unto God. I will submit myself to my Pastor as the Shepherd of the Flock in order to better interpret and practice the teachings of the Bible. I will endeavor to set an exact time each day to study my Bible.

_____   _____
                Name   Date

Questions to ask the Discipler

DAILY DECLARATION

Repeat Aloud Each Morning and Evening

The Bible was written for me and I can understand it.

MEMORY VERSE: *Study to shew thyself approved unto God, a workman that needeth not to be ashamed, rightly dividing the word of truth* (II Timothy 2:15).

CHECK BLOCK AFTER REPEATING

	Mon	Tues	Wed	Thurs	Fri	Sat	Sun
A.M.							
P.M.							

"HOW READEST THOU?"

It is one thing to read the Bible through,
Another thing to read to learn and do;
Some read it as their duty once a week,
But no instruction from the Bible seek;
While others read it with but little care,
With no regard to how they read nor where.
Some read to bring themselves into repute,
By showing others how they can dispute;
While others read because their neighbors do,
To see how long 'twill take to read it through;
Some read it for the wonders that are there,
How David killed a lion and a bear;
While others read it with uncommon care,
Hoping to find some contradictions there;
Some read as if it did not speak to them,
But to the people at Jerusalem.
One reads with father's specs upon his head,
And sees the thing just as his father said,
Some read to prove a pre-adopted creed;
Hence understand but little what they read;
For every passage in the book they bend,
To make it suit that all-important end.
Some people read, as I have often thought
To teach the book instead of being taught;
And some there are who read it out of spite.
I fear there are but few who read it right.
But read it prayerfully, and you will see,
Although men contradict, God's Words agree;
For what the early Bible prophets wrote,
We find that Christ and His apostles quote,
So trust no creed that trembles to recall,
What has been **penned by one and verified by all**.

Author Unknown

Lesson No. 5

YOU AND THE GOLDEN KEY

INTRODUCTION: This lesson is dedicated to the late Dr. Ben M. Bogard and his "Golden Key," which will help us to unlock or properly interpret the Scriptures.

Men have always followed simple rules in Bible interpretation. The Bible was written so that the common man could understand it. The famous translator, John Wycliffe, wrote the following rules of interpretation. He said, "It shall greatly help ye to understand scripture,

If thou **mark** not only what is **spoken** or **written,**
But **of whom** and **to whom,**
With **what words,** at **what time,** and **where,**
to **what intended,**
With **what circumstances,**
Considering **what goeth before,** and **what followeth.**"

I. **THE GOLDEN KEY**

   A. **This Golden Key is represented by four questions which will help unlock the scriptures.**

   They are:

   1. **Who** is speaking?

   2. To **whom** is he speaking?

   3. About **what** is he speaking?

   4. **When** was he speaking?

II. **WHO IS SPEAKING?**

   A. **Many may be surprised to learn that God does not do all the talking in the Bible.**

   1. Remember the Bible teaches that all scripture is given by inspiration of God. The Holy Spirit

directs and inspires the writer to give the account or conversation, but He does not inspire an individual to do wrong. He gives the account of the deed, but does not inspire the person to commit it.

2. In the Bible one finds verses uttered by God, angels of God, fallen angels, the devil, sinners, prophets, fools, harlots, and even a she-donkey.

3. It is very important to know "who is speaking," because it may be the words of the she-donkey or the devil who is being quoted.

III. TO WHOM IS HE SPEAKING?

A. There is much confusion, because people fail to realize that scripture was written by someone to someone.

1. **Not all statements** written in the Bible were written to a person living today, and you do not need to apply them to yourself directly,

2. **Sometimes** scripture is addressed to Israel as a Nation.

3. **Sometimes** scripture is written to a certain church in a certain town, and sometimes certain scripture is directed to all churches as a whole.

4. **While at other times,** scripture is written to a particular man under peculiar circumstances.

B. One thing a person should always remember when striving to understand a scripture is "To WHOM is he speaking?"

IV. ABOUT WHAT IS HE SPEAKING?

A. It has been said, "Anything can be proven by the Bible."

This is true only when the scriptures are taken from their proper setting and misapplied to a subject to which it was not meant to apply.

1. Once a man used the Bible to prove it was a sin to cut off a puppy's tail. The scripture? *"What God hath joined together let no man put asunder"* (Matthew 19:6).

2. Once a pastor startled his sleepy congregation by saying, "I can prove by the scriptures that you should all hang yourselves." The scripture? The one about Judas hanging himself, and the command, **"Go ye therefore and do likewise."**

V. WHEN WAS HE SPEAKING?

A. **The fourth question**, and many times a very important question, is "When was he speaking or about what time was this spoken?"

B. **A good example** of the time element in proper interpretation is found in Matthew 28:15.

The "this day" to which Matthew refers is until the time he wrote the book of Matthew, some thirty years after the resurrection of our Lord.

VI. THE BIBLE, NOT EMOTIONS, IS TO BE OBEYED!

A. Is the Bible the absolute authority?

The author presents this question, not because of any doubt he has of the authority of the Bible, but in order to make the reader think. Jesus said, *"THE SCRIPTURES CANNOT BE BROKEN"* (John 10:35). *"Heaven and earth* *shall pass away; but **my words shall not pass away***" (Luke 21:33).

Paul said, *"All scripture is given by inspiration"* (II Timothy 3:16-17), and will thoroughly furnish and equip the believer to every good WORK.

Are these statements true? Do you believe that God would place a book on the earth with explicit commandments and directions for mankind to follow? Or do you believe He would set up a system where the individual emotions of man would dictate what is right or wrong? Which would be the safest guide? A perfect book, which when properly interpreted, would give a safe guide to every man in every age; not a system where the feelings of the individual would dictate what is right or wrong.

1. **No true Bible believer would say.**

   Every person who knows anything about the flexibility of man's emotions and the infallibility of God's Holy and Perfect Word would have any problem with this question. No one would say that one should depend upon his feelings instead of obeying a plain command of the Bible. The apostles declared, **"Let God be true and all men liars"** (Romans 3:4). "We ought to obey God rather than man" (Acts 5:29).

2. **But there is a problem!**

   In Bible days, the Pharisees circumvented the plain commands of the law by claiming ultra scriptural gifts. Jesus rebuked them for their hypocrisy in Matthew 15:4-9. The plain command of the Bible, *"Honor thy Father and Mother,"* was set aside. These Pharisees would claim to believe the Bible, but they would disobey its plain teachings by claiming that it was a special gift, or that they had a special gift. They would say, "Yes, the Bible is true and one ought to obey it, but we have something you do not have; we are special. Jesus exposed their error and denounced their disruptive practice by saying in **vv 6-7,** *"Thus have ye made the commandment of God of none effect by your tradition. You hypocrites."*

VII. THE NEGATIVE AS WELL AS THE POSITIVE

We have noted the positive command to the believer to "rightly divide" the word of God. It is to show oneself a workman, which needs not to be ashamed when he stands before his creator.

A.   NOTICE THE POSITIVE once again

Note the word, workman. It did not say student, even though we are to be students of the word, BUT the purpose that one should study the Word is so he can be a proper workman for the Lord; not just to learn the word, but to do it.

B.   *"A good, acceptable and perfect will"*

Paul declares that God saved man for a purpose and that the believer is to PROVE what is that good, acceptable and perfect will for which he was saved. The POSITIVE command for rightly dividing the word is to find out what God saved that person to do. You are to STUDY, literally be very diligent or thoughtful—intense in your efforts to find your purpose and then give yourself to the task of "becoming a living sacrifice" (Romans 12:1) in your efforts to become a proper workman.

C.   The NEGATIVE command for rightly dividing the word

"Of these things put them in remembrance, charging them before the Lord that they strive not about words to no profit, BUT to the subverting of the hearers, study to show thyself approved unto God, a workman that needeth not to be ashamed, rightly dividing the word of truth. But shun profane and vain

babblings: for they will increase unto more ungodliness" (II Timothy 2:14-16)

1. **What is your purpose for learning the Bible?** It is to subvert, win, train, or develop the hearers.

2. **What is the purpose of learning to use the Bible?** It is to be a proper workman for the Lord. To be APPROVED by God, not man as you serve the Lord.

3. **One is not to study just to know,** but he is to study in order to follow the lifestyle and pattern, which God has laid out for his workers (children) to follow.

4. **He is not** to strive or learn the word to argue or try to straighten people out. Refuse profane and vain babbling. Study so you will be able to help people; never to show your skill or ability.

VIII TEST AND TRAIN YOURSELF

Test yourself by turning to a scripture at random, and find out **who is speaking** in it. You may have to read back a few verses or even turn back to the beginning of the book (epistle or letter), but study until you discover **who is speaking.**

After you have found out who is speaking, then proceed to the question, **to whom is he speaking?**

After you have determined the first two points, then proceed to the third question, **"about what is he speaking?"** Then, if applicable, answer the question of **when was he speaking.** By going through these four questions, you will be able to determine the true meaning of most verses.

PRACTICE, PRACTICE, PRACTICE!

Follow that routine over and over again until it is just a natural thing for you to ask yourself those four questions, as you read your Bible.

In order to obtain skill in rightly dividing the word of God, stay in the **NEW TESTAMENT** as you practice. There are 27 books in the New Testament. Twenty-one of these inspired books are epistles (letters), which were written by someone: to an individual, a local church, or to the saved (these are called general epistles [letters]). If you count Hebrews, the Apostle Paul wrote fourteen of these letters. The Apostle John wrote five of these letters, and Peter and Doctor Luke each wrote two. It is easier to determine these four questions in the New Testament than in the Old Testament, because the books are smaller. After you master the Golden Key (four key questions) in the New Testament, you will be confident to study anywhere in the Bible; but to be a good student of the Word, you must persevere.

AN EXAMPLE FROM ONE OF GOD'S GREATEST

George Mueller lived in England a little over 100 years ago. He set out to prove that **God would still answer prayer in "these last days."** He would have to be considered one of God's greatest and most successful "workmen." The author will close this section with some advice from that Spirit Filled Prayer Warrior who changed his generation.

THERE WAS A DAY WHEN I DIED:

Died to George Mueller: to his opinions, his desires, and his will;
Died to the world: to its approval or disapproval; and
Died to the acclaim or disclaim of his brethren.

Since that day, I have studied only to "show myself approved unto God."

This advice captures the true meaning of II Timothy 2:15: *"approved unto God,"* and *"rightly dividing the word of Truth...."* It catches the Spirit of God as well as the "Truth" or exactness of what the verse states. If you follow this example and advice, you too will have an impact on your generation.

IX. USE THE KEY TO BLESS HUMANITY

A. It is not enough for one to know how to study.

1. **James said** that one must be a doer of the Word and not a hearer only. It is not enough to learn that there is a true faith, which is presented in the Word of God, but we must practice it.

2. The Bible commands a person to study that he may rightly divide the Word of truth. By using these four questions, he will be able to unlock and understand the inspired Word of God.

3. This system will enable a person to understand the Bible well enough to tell others of the hope, that he has within himself, thus fulfilling God's greatest desire of spreading the truth.

Monday

(The Golden Key—Who is Speaking?)

1. The Golden Key will help us to _____ or properly interpret the _____.

2. The Bible was written so the _____ _____ could understand it.

3. The golden key is made up of _____ _____.

4. _____ _____ _____ is the first question one should ask in interpreting a scripture.

5. Name four different intities who are quoted in the Bible.
   (1)_____ (2)_____ (3)_____ _____
   (4)_____

Tuesday

(The Golden Key—To Whom Is He Speaking?)

1. Who is the most unlikely creature that speaks in the Bible?
   A _____ _____.

2. Why is there so much confusion in reading the Bible?

   _____ _____ ____ _____ _____

   _____ _____ _____ _____

   _____ ____ _____

3. What is the 2nd question in the Golden Key? ___ _____
   ____ ____ _____?

4. Sometimes the Scripture is addressed to _____ as a nation.

5. What must a person always remember if he is to interpret the Bible properly? ____ _____ ____ ____ _____?

Wednesday

(About What, & When Was He Speaking?)

1. What is the 3rd question in the Golden Key? _____
    _____ ____ ____ _____?

2. It has been said that _____ _____ _____
    _____ by the Bible.

3. When is this statement true? _____ _____
    _____ _____ _____ _____ _____
    _____ _____ _____.

4. What is the 4th question in the Golden Key? _____
    _____ ____ _____?

5. Which question is the Key to understanding Matthew
    28:15? _____

Thursday

(The Bible, Not Emotions—Section A & B)

1. A perfect book when properly _____ would
    be a _____ _____ to every man.

2. The Pharisees circumvented the plain _____ of the
    law by claiming special _____ _____.

3. These Pharisees would claim to _____ _____
    _____ but would disobey its plain teachings.

4. Note the word _____ it did not say student, even
    though we are to be _____ of the word.

5. The believer is to _____ what is that good,
    acceptable and _____ will for which he was
    saved.

68

Friday

(The NEGATIVE command through end of chapter)

1. What is the _____ of learning the Bible? To subvert, _____, train or _____ the hearers.

2. Stay in the _____ Testament as you practice in order to obtain _____ in rightly dividing the word of God.

3. The four Key Questions _____ will work anywhere, but you will have to _____ in order for it to do so.

4. He set out to prove that God would still answer _____ in these _____ days.

5. After George Mueller died to self, critics, and what his friends thought, he studied the Bible to show himself approved unto God a _____.

Having studied the Golden Key and found that the Bible was written for common men to understand, learn, and then teach others; I therefore enter into my lifelong study of God's Word, so I may share its truths with others.

_____   _____
                Name   Date

Questions to ask the Discipler:

DAILY DECLARATION

Repeat Aloud Each Morning and Evening

I will please God and strengthen myself by studying the Bible, His word, each day of my life.

MEMORY VERSE: *"Thy word havie I hid in mine heart, that I might not sin against thee"* (Psalms 119:11).

CHECK BLOCK AFTER REPEATING

	Mon	Tues	Wed	Thurs	Fri	Sat	Sun
A.M.							
P.M.							

WHY ARE YOU ON THIS EARTH?

You didn't ask to come in,
You won't be here long.
You were born with a nature to sin,
Alas, **you** will soon be gone!

So why are **you** here?
What's life all about?
You had better start thinking,
Because soon **you**'ll be going out!

To lose one's wealth is sad,
To lose one health is more,
But to never find one's purpose,
Is a loss that no man can restore!

Dr. James Wilkins

71

Lesson Number 6

GOD DESIGNED YOU TO WIN SOULS

INTRODUCTION: John 10:10 states that Jesus came that you may have abundant life. He didn't come that you may have just life but that you may live an abundant, victorious life. He designed you to win, to achieve, to live victoriously.

Many people read this verse – *"Jesus came that you may have life* [that's physical life] *and might have it* [life] *more abundantly* [that's eternal life]*."* This is not the proper interpretation of this verse. When the Bible refers to life it means eternal life, *"God has given to us eternal life, and this life is in His Son. He that hath the Son hath life* [what kind of life? eternal life]. *He that hath not the Son of God hath not life."* John the Baptist made it even plainer in John 3:36 when he said that a person who has not received eternal life, *"shall not see life; but the wrath of God abideth on him."* So the plain meaning of John 10:10 is that the believer has eternal, or never ending life, when he received Jesus Christ as his personal Savior. In addition to this He came that the believer may live an abundant, victorious, happy, successful, and fruitful Christian life.

I. WHAT IS THE FRUIT OF THE RIGHTEOUS?

    A. "The Fruit of the Righteous (Saved) is a tree of life; and he that winneth souls is wise" (Proverbs 11:30).

        1. GOD'S WORD DECLARES—Everything reproduces *"after its kind"* (Genesis 1:24).

            a. What is the fruit of an apple tree? Apples.

            b. What is natural when a young man and a young woman are married? Do they have to be superhuman, or an outstanding specimen of humanity in order to start a family? The obvious answer is, NO.

c. What is the fruit of cattle? The answers to these three questions are so absolutely plain that as evangelist Carl Hatch would say, "Even a 3rd grade retarded child could answer it."

d. Everything, which is alive, is to reproduce *"after its kind."*

2. **Who are the righteous** in Proverbs 11:30?

a. The Bible declares that a righteous person is one who has the imputed righteousness of Christ (a believer or a saved person) (Romans 4:3-5).

b. The word "righteous" is an old English word for saved.

c. In our modern, every day language, we would say "The fruit of the SAVED."

3. **The "Tree of Life"** is symbolic of eternal life.

The normal function of a saved person is to win souls. The tree does not produce fruit for its own benefit but for the benefit of others. The fruit of the saved is to win others to Christ. That is the normal function of a believer. That is exactly what Jesus commissioned His church to do (Matthew 28:18; Mark 16:15).

4. **God's interpretation** of *"The fruit of the righteous."*

a. One does not have to wonder about the proper meaning of fruit, for Proverbs 11:30 states that *"The fruit of the righteous* [saved] *is a tree of life,* so the fruit is eternal life."

73

b.   Proverbs 11:30, has two phases.

- The first phrase is *"The fruit of the the righteous is the tree of life."*

- The second phrase is, *"And he that winneth souls is wise,"* This shows us that when we win souls we give others the ability to have the fruit of life also.

II.   GOD HAS PROMISED THAT YOU CAN WILL SOULS.

A.   God's Divine Method.

"He that goeth forth and weepeth, bearing precious seed, shall doubtless come again with rejoicing, bringing his sheaves [fruit] *with him."* (Psalms 126:6).

1.   Notice, **'He'**

He is not a preacher.
He is not someone who has a gift of gab.
He is not someone who has a special calling.
He is just HE (anyone).

2.   Notice **'Shall'**

That's a definite promise to the one who goes (Burdened with the word*)*. *"Doubtless come again with rejoicing"* is an absolute promise from Almighty God.

3.   Notice **'with rejoicing'**

There are four descriptive terms of the job the soul-winner will have.

- *"Like them that dreamed"* (v. 1)

- *"Mouth filled with laughter"* (v. 2)

74

- *"Tongue with singing"* (v. 2)

4. *"Then said they among the heathen, The LORD hath done great things for them, and The LORD hath done great things for us; [whereof] we are glad."* (Psalms 126:2-3) Denotes success.

B. These Verses Promise the Abundant Life.

It states that anyone who goes with a concern for souls, with a message from the word:

1. Will doubtless come again with abundant, victorious life like them that dreamed, mouth filled with laughter, and tongue with singing.

2. Everyone noticed the blessing of God upon their life.They acknowledged God's blessing: *"Whereof we are glad."*

C. Five Simple Steps

You were not only designed to win, but God gave the simple steps for bearing fruit, which bring the abundant life.

The steps are:

1. Going – To the Lost

2. Weeping – Concerned

3. Sowing – The Message

4. Having Faith – A sure promise (Doubtless)

5. Rejoicing – Because of souls won.

III. GOD HAS CHOSEN THE WEAK THINGS

A. How are you feeling?

1. Do you feel like you "kain't"?

2. Do you feel like you are unable to win souls?

3. Do you feel that you have "Too big a Fear Problem?"

4. Do you feel that you have too much of an inferiority complex to overcome?

5. Do you feel that maybe you are just too dumb?

6. Do you feel that you are too self-conscious to win souls?

I HAVE GOOD NEWS FOR YOU .....

B. God Chose Little People.

That's right, God chooses little people, weak people, and people who have inferiority complexes to do great things. Read 1 Corinthians 1:27. He chose:

- A 17-year old boy – Joseph – To save his family Israel.

- A Jewish maiden – Esther – To deliver her whole country.

- A Hillbilly shepherd boy – David – to become Israel's greatest king.

- An ignorant fisherman – Peter – to become the first pastor and chief apostle.

- A little boy with a sack lunch,. a man with a rod, a man with an ox-goard, a widow with two mites, and YOU!!

C. But you say, "I feel so weak, so unworthy."

Good, that is a sure sign you can do it because God has chosen the weak things.

Paul went with tears, with fear and trembling, and he commanded us to work out our salvation (what we were saved to do: bear fruit [win souls]) with fear and trembling. So if you are scared, feel weak, feel foolish, or self-conscious, you have all the evidence of qualifying to become a great soul-winner (1 Corinthians 2:1-3; Acts 20:31; Philippians 2:12).

IV. HOW THE PEOPLE WHO WORKED WITH PAUL BE-CAME GREAT SOUL-WINNERS

A. Paul did It.

The Apostle Paul must have had a tremendous way of developing new converts. He would go into a heathen city, win souls to Christ, leave in a few months with a sound, highly trained, self-supporting church behind. This church was generally large in membership with pastors and deacons, and would continue on in a scriptural way even after the Apostle left. But HOW DID HE DO IT?

B. How he did it.

Paul used a sure-fire method which produced great results. Paul's method would produce great results today. His method was so simple that most completely overlook it – it had four simple steps. Those steps are:

1. He taught people how to witness in a public meeting.

2. He showed people how to witness in a public service (a soul-winning demonstration).

3. He taught a person how to witness in a home. He was a teacher-example to the young convert while out winning souls.

4.   He showed a person how to do it in a home (on the job training).

C.   **Paul's Method is Used Today.**

1.   Teach a person how to swim, then get into the water.

2.   First, there is driver's education, then there is driver's training.

3.   He taught the principles of soul-winning and then he showed them how in a soul-winning demonstration.

4.   He would take one student out, explain the procedure, and then perform what he explained.

5.   He would do this until his student had learned sufficiently; then the student would in turn, become a teacher. Paul would take another new convert and develop him using this same procedure.

6.   If the convert was slower, Paul took more time. If he learned more rapidly, Paul took less time. This method still works today.

V.   YOU CAN BECOME A GREAT SOUL-WINNER

A.   **You are to Grow in Grace.**

1.   In II Peter 3:18, Peter tells the disciples *"To grow in grace and knowledge"*. This means to continue to grow in grace and knowledge.

2.   A little girl of five years of age cannot do what her big sister of fifteen years of age can do, but through the process of natural growth, she may grow up and exceed her big sister in many ways.

3. You may not be able to witness and win souls now, but you can grow into a mature, fruitful Soul-Winner.

B. I Can Do All Things Through Christ.

Paul said he could do all things through Christ who strengthened or helped him (Philippians 4:13).

1. Is God a respecter of persons? NO! (Acts 10:34).

2. God's grace can help you to do all things. Especially a natural thing which He designed you to do.

3. That natural thing is the Fruit of the Saved, Soul-Winning.

C. We are to walk by faith.

Walk by Faith means, submit yourself to your pastor to be trained (with fear and trembling as a Soul-Winner).

D. Witnessing was designed by God for all of God's children.

Witnessing was designed so everyone could learn to do it. Witnessing is one of the simplest, easiest things for a person to do. Once you learn the simple steps in witnessing, it becomes a natural way of life.

E. Three Basic Principles.

All a person has to do is, learn to do three basic techniques.

1. One must learn how to get into a soul-winning (spiritual) conversation.

2. One must learn what to say in a soul-winning conversation (one plan).

3. One must learn what to do at the close of a soul-winning conversation.

One will begin to learn these principles in our next lesson.

MONDAY

(Introduction)

1. He designed you to _____, to _____, to _____
   _____.

2. Many people read John 10:10, *"Jesus came that you may
   have life* [_____ _____ _____] which is a
   wrong interpretation.

3. What type of life does the believer receive when he is
   saved? _____ _____

4. In addition to eternal life, what type of life has Jesus
   designed us to live? _____ _____ _____
   _____ and _____.

5. John the Baptist said a person either had eternal life or the
   _____ of God _____ on him.

TUESDAY

(The Fruit of the Righteous)

1. Everything reproduces after _____ _____ (Genesis
   1:24-25).

2. The word *"righteous"* is an Old English word for _____.

3. *"Tree of life"* is symbolic of _____ _____.

4. The _____ function of a saved person is to win
   _____.

5. God's interpretation of the Fruit of the Righteous is a tree
   of life and He that _____ _____ is _____.

WEDNESDAY
(God Has Promised)

1. He, that is not _____ _____, or someone with a gift of _____, or someone with a special _____, but it is he (_____).

2. *"Shall"* means an absolute promise from _____ God.

3. The soul-winner has the fullness of joy which the Psalmist described as _____ them that dreamed, mouth filled with _____, tongue with _____, and everyone commented that God has done _____ things for them whereof they were _____.

4. God not only designed the saved to win souls but gave _____ _____ _____ to bearing fruit.

5. The steps are _____, _____, _____ (doubtless) _____, _____ because of souls won.

THURSDAY
(God Chose—How the People)

1. God has chosen the _____ things.

2. Paul went with _____, with fear and _____ and commanded us to _____ out our salvation with _____ and _____.

3. If you feel weak, foolish, self-conscious, then you have all the _____ of qualifying to become a great _____- _____.

4. Paul taught them _____ _____ _____ in a public service.

5. He showed a person how to do it in a home (on the _____ _____).

6. Paul's method of training soul-winners still _____ today.

FRIDAY
(You Can Become)

1. You can become a _____ soul-winner.
2. You may not be able to witness and _____ souls now, but you can _____ _____ ____ _____, _____ _____ - _____.
3. Is God a respecter of persons? _____
4. Walk by faith means submit yourself to _____ _____ to be trained (with fear and trembling) as a _____ - _____.
5. Once one learns the simple steps in witnessing it becomes a _____ _____ of life.

I accept that the Bible teaches that I was designed by God to win souls. I will therefore submit to the training program of our church as a trainee, silent partner in their on the job training program. I will attend at least one visitation service each week. I now dedicate myself to becoming a Fruit Bearing Christian.

_____ _____
Name   Date

Questions to ask the discipler:

DAILY DECLARATION

Repeat Aloud Each Morning And Evening

God's purpose for my life is for me to become a happy, victorious, overcoming, fruitful Christian.

MEMORY VERSE: *"The fruit of the righteous is a tree of life; and he that winneth souls is wise"* (Proverbs 11:30).

CHECK BLOCK AFTER REPEATING

	Mon	Tues	Wed	Thurs	Fri	Sat	Sun
A.M.							
P.M.							

IT WAS JUST A VISIT

One day I rang a doorbell
In a casual sort of way.
T'was not a formal visit,
And there wasn't much to say.

I don't remember what I said—
It matters not I guess—
I found a heart in hunger;
A soul in deep distress.

He said I came from Heaven,
And I often wondered why;
He said I came to see him,
When no other help was nigh.

It meant so little to me,
To knock on a stranger's door;
But it meant heaven to him,
And God's peace for-ever-more.

John R. Rice, D.D.

Lesson Number 7

THE COUNT DOWN METHOD

"A Simple Soul-Winning Plan"

FIVE!   **Five Approach Questions**

FOUR!   **Four Spiritual laws** contained in four scriptures

THREE!   **Three possibilities** after the soul talk is given

TWO!   **Two people on a team.** For best results, go two by two. Two separate people each with a job to do.

ONE!   **One supreme purpose** of a soul-winning effort is to learn to work with the Holy Spirit in presenting the plan to the lost in a way which will bring him to Christ.

INTRODUCTION: God wanted everyone to win souls, so He made it so simple that ANYONE can understand how to do it. **There are only three parts** to a soul-winning effort.

1.   **The opening** of the plan or the approach.

2.   **The body** or the message during the soul talk.

3.   **The termination** of the talk or the close.

After a short period of informal conversation (about 5 to 10 minutes) in which one breaks the ice with the prospect, the soul-winner should begin his opening of the soul-winning talk. The **OPENING contains five approach QUESTIONS.** These approach questions bring the conversation to the main body of the soul-talk, the message.

The message centers around **four spiritual laws**, which are found in four scriptures.

1.   **The fact of sin** (Romans 3:23).

2.   **The consequences** of sin (Romans 6:23a).

3.   **The remedy** for sin (Romans 5:8).

4.   **The individual response** (Romans 10:13)

When these four principles are presented to the lost, there are three possibilities or reactions to the witness.

1.   He **will want** to be saved.

2.   He **will not want** to be saved.

3.   He **will hesitate** in making a decision.

A personal worker simply has to learn what to do in these three situations.

The Bible pattern in soul-winning is for the soul-winning team to consist of two people. One to do the **witnessing** while the other serves in **assisting** the soul-winner.

The final principle is the **ONE SURPEME** purpose of the visit, which is to work with the Holy Spirit in presenting the plan of salvation to the lost.

TAKE TIME TO MASTER

1.   The **five approach questions**,

2.   How to apply the **four simple scriptures** and;

3.   Learn what to do when he receives one **of the three reactions.** If he masters these 3 principles, then he can and will become a great soul-winner.

I.   **THE OPENING OF THE PLAN**

   A.   **Begin with five to ten minutes of conversation, which is designed to make the prospect like you.**

1. **Talk on his interest level.** In order to be effective in witnessing, one must learn to control the conversation. He does this by asking questions, which will keep the prospect talking about things, in which he is interested.

2. In visitation, one takes the fear and the distress out of witnessing by sending an **S.O.S.** The letters S.O.S. each stand for an area of conversation which will lead the prospect to the object of the visit which is presenting Christ (the message).

   > **S. – Self interest** – hobbies, vacations, and family interest

   > **O. – Occupation** – work, homemaker, or student

   > **S. – Soul-winning message**

3. **The opening** is designed where the soul-winner makes a transition from a friendly visit and an enjoyable fellowship in which the prospect talks on his level of interest to a soul-winning effort. This is the point where many soul-winners or would-be soul-winners choke up and are unable to make a smooth transition to a visit where the message of salvation is given. One can learn to make a smooth transition to the message by asking **five simple questions**. The soul-winner has been asking questions, which have kept the prospect talking on his interest level. The approach questions are so automatic and in harmony with your designed, controlled conversation that the prospect has consented to the soul-winning message without resentment, and in most cases, is anxious to listen.

A. The Five Approach Questions

1. **You are interested in Spiritual things aren't you?** It is better to say, I can see by the plaque on the wall..., by our conversation..., by the Bible there that you are interested in spiritual things, aren't you?

2. **Have you ever considered that you need eternal life?**

3. **If you should die today, do you know for sure that you would go to Heaven?**

4. **You would like to know, wouldn't you?** "Well, yes, I would like to know."

5. **If I could take your Bible and show you how you could know for sure, would you consider doing something about it?**

   Upon his affirmative answer, you reach inside your pocket or hand bag and pull out your concealed weapon, the New Testament, or you present your Bible and proceed to show him the message.

A. Master the approach questions.

In mastering the approach questions, one will eliminate many questions, which the prospect will ask. They are one of the vital parts of witnessing, and **they must be** MASTERED!

II. THE MESSAGE CONTAINED IN THE FOUR SPIRITUAL LAWS

The message is found in four simple scriptures, the first scripture is:

A. THE FIRST SPIRITUAL PRINCIPLE IS THE FACT OF SIN:

"For all have sinned and come short of the glory of God" (Romans 3:23).

1. The Word, "all", places us "ALL IN THE SAME BOAT."

    This means that I **have sinned.** That means **the finest person in the world has sinned.** That means **"YOU" have sinned.**

2. YOU HAVE HEARD OF THE TEN COMMAND-MENTS, HAVEN'T YOU?

    Most people are trying to keep the Ten Commandments, and by doing so, they hope to go to Heaven when they die! In reality, every normal adult has broken most, if not all, of these commandments. **For example:**

    a. One of the commandments states, *"Thou shalt not take God's name in vain"* (swear).

    b. Another says, *"Honor thy Father and Mother"* (obey them).

    c. Still a third states, *"Thou shalt not bear false witness:* (lie).

3. IN ORDER TO HELP YOU SEE THAT ALL HAVE SINNED, may I ask you this question? HOW MANY BANKS would a man have to rob before he became a bank robber? By the same logic, one lie would make a person a liar, while one sin would make a person a sinner.

B. **THE SECOND SPIRITUAL PRINCIPLE IS THE CONSEQUENCES OF SIN:**

"For the wages of sin is death" (Romans 6:23).

1. There are two key words in this verse, WAGES AND DEATH.

Wages means a payoff, penalty or what one gets for being a sinner. Death means separation.

2. **HAVE YOU EVER BEEN TO A FUNERAL?**

The body is lying there in the casket. The real person has been separated from his body. That is physical death.

3. **WHEN YOU DIE** GOD WANTS TO REACH RIGHT DOWN AND TAKE YOU RIGHT INTO HEAVEN.

But if you are still in your sins, have never been reconciled, born again, or saved; God will say to you, Your sins separate you from me, your sins shut you out of Heaven.

4. **THERE ARE ONLY TWO ETERNAL PLACES**.

Heaven, where God is, and Hell, a literal place of fire, pain, and separation. The wages (pay off), for being a sinner is eternal separation from God in Hell.

C. **THE THIRD SPIRITUAL PRINCIPLE IS THE REMEDY FOR SIN:**

"But God commendeth His love toward us in that while we were yet sinners, Christ died for us." (Romans 5:8).

1. **GOD HAD THIS PROBLEM TO SOLVE**.

You acknowledged that you were a sinner, and the Bible states that if you pay for your sin, then you will be separated from God eternally in Hell. How can God send you to Hell and at the same time take you to Heaven?

91

2. **TO ILLUSTRATE THIS PROBLEM.**

Let me ask you this question. "HOW CAN I BE IN TWO PLACES AT THE SAME TIME?" You say, "You can't be." God had to work out how I could pay for my sin by dying (going to Hell), and yet to be forgiven and go to Heaven. IT SEEMED IMPOSSIBLE! His solution! If someone would die in my place and pay for my sins, then God would forgive me and take me to Heaven for that person's sake.

3. **THAT'S WHAT JESUS WAS DOING ON THE CROSS.**

He was dying as your substitute, paying for your sins "...Christ died for you" or in your place.

4. **LET ME ASK YOU, "HAVE YOU EVER RECEIVED A TRAFFIC TICKET?"**

Imagine that I received a traffic ticket, appeared before the judge who pronounced judgment upon me by saying, "It will take $75.00 or five days in jail to satisfy the State of Texas." If I did not have any money and could not pay my fine, the State of Texas would still be satisfied if someone else paid this ticket for me. THAT IS WHAT JESUS DID ON THE CROSS FOR YOU. He was paying your SIN TICKET, satisfying THE LAW OF GOD, which demanded payment.

D. **THE FOURTH SPIRITUAL PRINCIPLE IS THE INDIVIDUAL RESPONSE:**

"For whosoever shall call upon the name of the Lord shall be saved" (Romans 10:13).

1. **THERE ARE TWO KEY WORDS IN THIS VERSE.**

They are "WHOSOEVER" and "SAVED" (redeemed from Hell). WHOSOEVER means you! It means anyone who calls upon the name of the Lord. Jesus died and paid the sin debt for every man. The word SAVED means delivered from Hell.

2. **"SHALL CALL UPON"** means pray or ask the Father.

What this verse says is that "If you really understand that you are a sinner, that you are going to Hell, and that Jesus literally died in your place (paid for your sin), and you call upon the name of the Lord (ASK him to save you for Jesus' sake), HE WILL SAVE YOU FROM HELL.

3. JESUS AND HIS FATHER REACHED THIS AGREEMENT.

If Jesus died in your place and paid for your sin, then God, the Father, would accept His death as full payment for your sins and save you from Hell, if you ask Him to Save you for Jesus' sake. In Heaven, Jesus is seated beside His Father reminding Him of this agreement and pleading the sinners case right now. He is saying, "I died for him, I paid for his sin, now FORGIVE HIM AND SAVE HIM FOR MY SAKE." God will honor His word and save every sinner who turns from his sin, and earnestly desires and asks for the forgiveness of sin. If you haven't already done so, bow your head and pray this simple prayer right now. "Dear Lord, I acknowledge my sin. I accept you as my Lord and Savior, and from this day on I will live for you. In Jesus' name, Amen."

III. THREE POSSIBILITIES AT THE CLOSE

The plan of salvation has been given, now the prospect will react in one of three ways.

A. The Most Vital Time in the Soul Talk.

1. This is the most important phase of the presentations, so master the close.

2. After you have presented a positive, confident image to the prospect in your approach question and in presenting the four spiritual laws, do not become negative or falter here.

3. Go right into your effort by asking the prospect if you may have a word of prayer.

A. Enter Into Your Close By:

1. Ask the prospect these questions again:

   a. You understand you have sinned, don't you?

   b. If you paid for your sins you would be eternally separated from God?

   c. That Jesus paid your sin ticket

   d. That He is pleading your case right now to His Father.

   e. That God will save you if you will ask Him in Jesus' name.

2. **Now, I honestly believe that God has spoken to your heart.**

a. Before I **leave I would like to have a word of prayer**. You wouldn't mind if I prayed would you?

3. **Bow your head and pray**.

   a. **Pray the four Spiritual Laws** to him again using his name.

   b. Then ask him to take you by the hand and **repeat this simple prayer**.

   > "Father, I know I have sinned. If I died, I would go to Hell. Please forgive me and save me. Jesus, come into my heart. I accept you now and I trust you to take me to Heaven when I die. Amen."

4. **Say**, "You really meant that didn't you?"

   a. If he says, "Yes, I did."

   b. You ask, "What did God say he would do if you ask him." Answer: Save Me.

   c. You say, "Can God lie?" Answer: "NO."

   d. You ask, "Then according to the Bible, where would you go if you should die?" Answer: "Heaven."

   e. You say, "Great! Isn't that wonderful?" Now take a few minutes to rejoice with the new convert.

5. **FINAL INSTRUCTIONS** TO THE NEW CONVERT.

   a. Get him to tell someone of his decision of Salvation.

   b. Show him 1 John 5:10-13.

c. Lead him in a final prayer and have him promise God that he will be in Church Sunday.

d. Make plans to pick him up and take him to church.

e. Introduce him around, sit with him and encourage him to go down and make a Public Profession.

MONDAY
(Introduction)

1. The countdown method is a _____ soul-winning _____.

2. There are _____ approach questions, _____ spiritual laws, _____ possibilities at the close, _____ on a team, and _____ supreme purpose in a soul-winning effort.

3. The informal visit, which is called S.O.S., is recommended to be _____ to _____ minutes in length.

4. The _____ is contained in five approach _____.

5. The message centers around _____ principles which are found in _____ scriptures.

TUESDAY
(The Opening of the Plan)

1. When you have DISTRESS think of ____. ____. ____.

2. The first "S" in the S.O.S. stands for _____ _____.

3. The "O" in the S.O.S. stands for _____.

4. The final "S" in the S.O.S. stands for _____ - _____ _____.

5. The first approach question is, "Are _____ _____ in _____ _____?".

97

6. If you should die today, do you _____ for sure that you would go to _____?

WEDNESDAY
(The Message)

1. The first spiritual law is the _____ of _____.
2. The _____ of sin is the second spiritual law.
3. The _____ for sin deals with God's love and provision for the sinner.
4. The final spiritual law is the _____ _____.
5. Jesus is seated _____ His Father reminding Him of this _____.

THURSDAY
(Three Possibilities)

1. There are three possibilities at the _____.
2. The prospect will react in _____ of _____ ways.
3. The close is the most _____ time of the soul talk.
4. This is the most _____ phase of the presentation, so _____ the close.
5. After a positive soul-winning effort do _____ become _____ or falter at the close.

FRIDAY

(Enter Into the Close)

1. Give the prospect the opportunity of making his own _____ by offering to have _____ with him.

2. Pray the _____ spiritual laws to him _____ using his name.

3. Say, "You really _____ _____ didn't you?" Never ask him "How do you feel?"

4. According to the _____ where would you go if you should die, is the proper question to ask after he has prayed.

5. What portion of scripture should you read in order to give him assurance? ___ _____ ___:_____.

6. Make an _____ to pick him up for church. Sit with him in church. Go _____ with him for the public _____.

Having studied this lesson on the "Simple Plan in Soul-Winning," I will work at, memorize, and do my best to learn how to share my faith in my daily life. I will submit myself to the pastor to become a silent partner-trainee in MY CHURCH VISITATION PROGRAM. I will attend at least one visitation service-training session per week when able to do so and as my church makes such sessions available to me.

_____   _____
Name   Date

DAILY DECLARATION

Repeat Aloud Each Morning And Evening

I will master the "Count Down Method" and win souls.

MEMORY VERSE: *"I can do all things through Christ, which strengthen me"* (Philippians 4:13).

CHECK BLOCK AFTER REPEATING

	Mon	Tues	Wed	Thurs	Fri	Sat	Sun
A.M.							
P.M.							

Questions to ask my discipler:

MY COMMITMENT AS A CHRISTIAN

I'M A PART OF THE FELLOWSHIP OF THE UNASHAMED. I HAVE THE POWER OF THE HOLY SPIRIT. THE DYE HAS BEEN CAST. I HAVE STEPPED OVER THE LINE. THE DECISION HAS BEEN MADE. **I'M A DISCIPLE OF HIS.** I WON'T LOOK BACK, LET UP, SLOW DOWN, BACK AWAY, OR BE STILL. I NO LONGER NEED PRE-EMINENCE, PROSPERITY, POSITION, PROMOTIONS, PLAUDITS, OR POPULARITY. I DON'T HAVE TO BE RIGHT, FIRST, TOPS, RECOGNIZED, PRAISED, REGARDED, OR REWARDED.

MY PAST IS REDEEMED, MY PRESENT MAKES SENSE, MY FUTURE IS SECURE. I'M FINISHED AND DONE WITH LOW LIVING, SIGHT WALKING (NOT WALKING BY FAITH), SMALL PLANNING, SMOOTH KNEES (NOT PRAYING), COLORLESS DREAMS, TAMED VISIONS, MUNDANE TALKING, CHEAP LIVING, AND DWARFED GOALS.

MY FACE IS SET, MY GAIT IS FAST, MY GOAL IS HEAVEN, AND MY MISSION CLEAR. I CANNOT BE BOUGHT, COMPROMISED, DETOURED, LURED AWAY, TURNED BACK, DELUDED, OR DELAYED. I WILL NOT FLINCH IN THE FACE OF SACRIFICE, HESITATE IN THE PRESENCE OF THE ADVERSARY, OR MEANDER IN THE MAZE OF MEDIOCRITY.

I WON'T GIVE UP, SHUT UP, LET UP, UNTIL I HAVE STAYED UP, STORED UP, PRAYED UP, PAID UP, AND PREACHED UP FOR THE CAUSE OF CHRIST. **I AM A DISCIPLE OF JESUS,** AND WHEN HE COMES FOR HIS OWN, HE WILL HAVE NO PROBLEM RECOGNIZING ME. **MY BANNER WILL BE CLEAR!**

Written by a young African pastor and tacked on the wall of his house.

Lesson No. 8

PRAYER

"TALKING TO YOUR FATHER"

INTRODUCTION: *"Whereby we cry, Abba, Father."* (Romans 8:15).

I.   **THE PROPER VIEW OF GOD**

A.   **God is the God of Abraham, Isaac, and Jacob.**

1.   Many people view God as living in a far off place, who is the God of Bible characters, and who is not too interested in their personal life and problems. This is completely wrong.

2.   God is interested in the smallest details of his children's lives.

a.   If He knows the number of hairs on ones head, He is concerned (Matthew 10:30).

b.   If He sees the little sparrow when it falls, He is concerned with His children's needs (Matthew 10:29).

c.   Paul said that He is touched with our infirmities, which means the little problems as well as one's life shattering problems (Hebrews 4:15).

B.   **Prayer comes from the Greek word "Aiteo," which means to ask, or asking.**

1.   The verse, Romans 8:15, gives the spirit of prayer—*"Whereby we cry, Abba,"* which is the dearest term for Father. It is not the formal term, Father, BUT THE ENDEARING TERM "DADDY."

It is used like a little child looking up into her father's face and pleading, "Daddy, please?".

2.   Jesus instructs the disciples to pray (Matthew 6:1-18). The term "Father" is FOUND TEN TIMES in those 18 verses. This repetition of the word "father" shows that when one prays, one should not think of some far off, impersonal God who doesn't care. He is to talk to His "Daddy."

II.   HOW SHOULD A PERSON PRAY?

A.   The beginning of the prayer.

The Bible teaches us to begin by addressing God in a respectful, reverent way, "Our Father," or "Our Heavenly Father," etc.

B.   The prayer itself.

After addressing God as your Father, the person then asks God for the petition or the desires that he wants.

1.   Things to Pray for:

Pray for wisdom,
Pray for the lost,
Pray for daily needs such as a job,
Pray for daily bread or food,
Pray for the sick,
Pray for the pastor,
Pray for people in authority,
Pray for people who give you a hard time,
Pray!

2.   Is it right to beg God for things?

The word supplication means begging. This teaches that God encourages his children to be persistent in asking Him for things.

C. The close of the prayer.

We are commanded to pray in Jesus' name.

In Jesus' name means by His authority. The child
of God has been authorized by Jesus to come boldly
into God's presence and present his needs (Hebrews
4:16).

1. In Jesus' name means—for Jesus' sake. (Do it
    Father), not because we have the authority to
    pray, but because it will please Jesus to do it for
    us.

2. There is only one name by which believers are au-
    thorized to pray. *"For [there is] one God, and one
    mediator between God and men, the man Christ
    Jesus"* (I Timothy 2:5).

    The word, "Mediator" means intercessor, go-
    between, or authorized.

III. THE A B C's OF PRAYER

Matthew 7:7 teaches that there are 3 parts to successful
praying. These three parts are

- *"Ask, and it shall be given you,"*

- *"Seek, and ye shall find,"* and

- *"Knock and it shall be opened unto you."*

A. Ask, and it shall be given you.

1. The asking part of prayer is what one generally
    thinks is prayer. It is the first part of successful
    praying and asking God.

2. The Bible teaches that one ought to have a
    regular time for prayer.

a. The apostles had a set time to pray—"At the hour of prayer" (Acts 3:1).

b. Daniel went into his house and prayed three times a day (Daniel 6:10).

c. A Christian ought to have a regular place of prayer. Jesus commanded, *"enter into thy closet"* (Matthew 6:6).

B. Seek, and you shall find.

This means that when one asks God for something, he is to put legs on his prayers. He is to do his part in bringing the prayer to pass.

Pray for the lost, then tell someone what Jesus did for you.

C. Knock and it shall be opened.

1. This means that one should be persistent in his praying.

2. The example of knocking illustrates persistence. In the parable found in Luke 11:1-13, there is a man who had company but no food to feed them. He went to the storekeeper and beat on the door until he received the bread.

3. The Bible teaches for God's children to keep praying, seeking, praying, seeking; until they obtain what they are praying for.

IV. THE EXAMPLE OF PRAYER IN THE BIBLE.

A. "Lord, teach us to pray."

This sincere request by the Apostles shows the importance they attached to prayer. They never asked Him to teach them to preach, to witness, or to give; but they DID BESEECH HIM TO TEACH THEM TO PRAY.

Many people get the wrong meaning to this verse by misreading it. They read it to say, "Lord, teach us how to pray." But the word "how" is not found in the verse. The Apostles wanted Jesus to teach them the application of prayer, not how to pray.

B. **Prayer in the Lives of the Apostles.**

After Jesus had spent three and a half years preparing the Apostles for the place of leadership in the early churches, He ascended to heaven. God blessed their efforts, and thousands were saved and added to the church. As their duties and problems were multiplied, trouble began to appear in the church. The Apostles felt that they were being cheated out of precious time and knew they were out of their place of service. Something had to be done, and something was done.

> "...It is not fitting that we should leave the word of God, and serve tables. Wherefore, brethren, look among you for seven men of honest report, full of the Holy Ghost and wisdom, whom we may appoint over this business. But we will give ourselves continually to prayer, and to the ministry of the word" (Acts 6:2-4).

What was their biggest objection? Where did they think they were being cheated? They wanted to be freed from some of the lesser responsibilities, so they could give themselves "continually to prayer and to the ministry of the word." **Notice**: ...prayer, then the ministry of the Word. Prayer came first in their lives.

C. **Prayer in the life of Christ.**

1. Christ was a great example. The importance of prayer can be seen by the prominent place that it held in the life of Christ. Although He walked on the earth, it seemed that Jesus lived in the presence of God who was in Heaven; He spent much time in prayer. Most of His public deeds and all of His critical moments were preceded by

prayer. The following is the best summary of the prayer life of Jesus that the author has seen.

2.   Jesus prayed:

- He prayed often. Prayer filled His life.
- He prayed before He faced any great task or trial.
- He prayed in public.
- He prayed in secret (often all night, some-times alone, and sometimes with His disciples) (Matthew 6:6; Luke 6:22).
- He put a high premium on secret prayer (Matthew 6:6).
- He practiced intercessory prayer (John 17:9-26).
- He promised the power of the Holy Spirit in answer to prayer (Luke 11:13).
- He taught that a sinner could pray for his own salvation (Luke 18:3).

3.   Jesus is a great example.

In order to further understand the importance of prayer in the life of Jesus Christ, one must realize this amazing fact: He not only **WAS** A GREAT EXAMPLE in prayer, but HE **IS** A GREAT EXAMPLE in prayer. Prayer is the most important part of His ministry today. Many believe that the work of Christ ended upon His death, but it did not! As far as His atoning work was concerned, it was finished; but Hebrews 7:25 pictures Christ as a very busy man. It says, *"Wherefore he is able also to save them to the uttermost that come unto God by him, seeing he ever liveth to make intercession for them."* This statement is backed up by the Apostle Paul in Romans 8:34. *"Who [is] he that condemneth? [It is] Christ that died, yea rather, that is risen again, who is even at the right hand of God, who also maketh intercession for us."*

4.   Fellowship with Christ.

     If one wants to follow Christ, he has to walk in the light, as He is the light. *"But if we walk in the light, as he is in the light, we have fellowship one with another, and the blood of Jesus Christ his Son cleanseth us from all sin* (I John 1:7). One must follow the light to Gethsemane, lift up his face, and pray!

V.   YOUR PRAYER LIFE

A.   The quiet time

Every successful Christian must have a quiet time set aside in his daily life for prayer and communion with God.   Jesus called this quiet time, *"enter into they closet."*

B.   A prayer list

Previously it has been pointed out that one cannot pray in general terms and expect to succeed.   He should have definite names and projects to call out before God. If it is necessary to make a grocery list before going shopping, how much more necessary it should be to have a prayer list to bring before God. Aaron, the High Priest of Israel, wore the names of the twelve tribes of Israel upon his shoulders to keep them ever before the eyes of God.

C.   Pray for power

It takes the power of God to lead a lost man to Christ.   God alone can touch, convict, bring to repentance, and save a sinner. But God's method in reaching the lost has always been by empowering men to do this vital job.   Each Christian should pray for power and favor toward unsaved humanity.

1.   Some reasons for failure. The following reasons are given in the Book of James as elements that

hinder prayer. Such reasons as regarding iniquity in one's heart and being unforgiving in one's heart toward a brother will not be enlarged upon, but the author will present the seven reasons which are found in James 4:1-11 for hindered prayer.

a. *"Ye ask not,"* verse two.

b. *"Ye ask amiss,"* verse three. You ask for something to satisfy your own desire.

c. *"Friendship of the world,"* verse four.

d. *"God resiseth the proud,"* verse six.

e. *"Failing to resist the devil,"* verse eight

f. *"Failing to draw nigh to God;"* living too far away from Him, verse eight.

g. *"Speaking evil of the brethren, therefore, I will not hear you when you pray"* (v.11).

D. In order to live right, one must pray right.

Unless a person begins his Christian life by having a definite time for prayer and guards that time, he will soon slip into the habit of NOT praying. When this happens, sin will begin to crowd into his life. He will lose the joy of salvation. He will lose his zeal for God's work. Please! Please! Grasp the importance of prayer. Develop good prayer habits and YOU WILL LIVE RIGHT AND SUCCEED FOR GOD!

Monday (The Proper View)

1. Many view God as a God who is living in a _____ _____

    _____.

2. *"He is touched with our _____"* (Hebrews **4:15**).

3. What does "aiteo" mean? ____ _____

4. How is the term "aba" used? Like a little child looking up into her father's face and pleading, " _____ _____?"

5. How many times is the word "father" found in Matthew 6:1-18? _____

Tuesday (How to Pray)

1. How do you start the prayer? One starts the prayer by addressing _____ in a _____, _____

    _____.

2. What does the word supplication mean? _____

3. What does in Jesus' name means? ____ _____ _____

4. In Jesus' name also means ____ _____ _____

5. How many mediators are there? _____

6. What does mediator mean? _____ ___ _____

    ___ _____.

Wednesday (The A B C's)

1. What are the three steps in Biblical prayer? 1. _____

    2. _____ 3. _____

2. Seek and ye _____ _____

3. You ask God for something, and then you put _____ ___

110

_____ prayers.

4. Knock means to be _____ in your prayers.

5. The Bible teaches to keep on _____, _____
_____ _____, until you obtain what you
are praying for.

Thursday (Examples of Prayer)

1. The apostles asked Jesus to teach them _____ _____

2. What was first in the lives of the apostles? _____

3. Jesus _____ a great example in prayer.

4. Jesus _____ a great example in prayer today.

5. How can you have better fellowship with Christ in your life?
To _____.

Friday (Your Prayer Life)

1. Every Christian ought to have a _____ _____
each day.

2. Jesus called this quiet time by the phrase _____ _____
_____ _____.

3. What definite request should the believers ask God for?

_____.

4. You have not because ye _____ _____ (James 4:2).

5. You have not because you _____ evil of the
brethren.

Having studied this lesson on prayer, I commit to set aside a definite time each day for prayer, and to do all I can to have family prayer each day. I now make my prayer list and will pray for each of these requests every day. My private prayer time will be _____ each day.

_____ _____
Name   Date

DAILY DECLARATION

Repeat aloud each morning and evening

The same God who changed the course of History by answering prayer will answer my prayers also.

MEMORY VERSE: *"The effectual, fervent prayer of a righteous man availeth much.* (James 5:16).

Questions to ask my discipler:

CHECK BLOCK AFTER REPEATING

	Mon	Tues	Wed	Thurs	Fri	Sat	Sun
A.M.							
P.M.							

WHAT MOTIVATES YOUR GIVING?

Those who give with the right motive are always receiving and always have more to give. "...freely ye have received, freely give" (Matthew 10:8).

Some Give to get as much in return, **that is exchange!**

Some give in order to receive more, **that is covetousness!**

Some give expecting notice, **that is vanity!**

Some give to receive favor, **that is bribery!**

Some Give because God commands, **that is obedience!**

Some Give out of a heart of love, **that is compassion!**

One of the greatest lessons a Christian can learn is to work with the Holy Spirit. Some say, "I believe God can do it," but they do nothing to help the Lord in fulfilling His will. "Faith without works is dead..." (James 2:26).

When a person uses money to share God's truth with those who desire His will, God sees to it that the person gains much. "The liberal soul shall be fat..." (Proverb 11:25).

The great promises of God can only **become a reality** when one gives in the right Spirit. Whether one gives money, kind words, prayer, or encouragement, **everything depends upon one's motives**.

"Whether therefore you eat, or drink, or whatsoever ye do, **do all to the glory of God**" (I Corinthians 10:31).

Lesson Number Nine

HOW TO HAVE SOMETHING IN HEAVEN

WHEN YOU GET THERE

"He which soweth bountifully..." (II Corinthians 9:6)

INTRODUCTION: When billionaire Howard Hughes died, the common question was, "I wonder how much he left behind?" Thousands of column inches were given in speculation; radio and television commentators ran far and wide in their efforts to outguess the other expert on the question of how much Howard Hughes, the eccentric billionaire, left behind.   Finally, an insignificant, smallish, baldheaded accountant, who worked on the staff of the controlling board of one of Mr. Hughes' high corporations, gave a startling, accurate answer to this question, when he said, "He left it all, every red cent of it. He never took one copperhead with him."   Having read of the selfish, sinful, lustful life of Mr. Hughes for 35 years, I am sure that that answer was absolutely true. He left every red cent. He never took one copperhead with him ... but it didn't have to be that way.

Everyone has heard of someone who was spending money as though it were going out of style, and yet laugh at the cautioning of some parent, wife, or concerned person, and say, "You can't take it with you." But my friend, that is not true. One can take it with him.

Jesus commanded the Christian to lay up treasure in Heaven. This command to lay up treasure in Heaven would not have been given unless it was possible to lay up, or save one's treasures in Heaven. One CAN TAKE IT WITH HIM, or, to say it another way, one can send it on before him. Read the plain command from the lips of Jesus as found in Matthew 6:19-20.

"Lay not up for yourselves treasures upon Earth, where moth nor rust doth corrupt, and where thieves break through and steal, BUT LAY UP FOR YOURSELVES (Who? For the preacher? For someone else? No, for yourselves.)   *TREASURES IN HEAVEN* (that's for eternity), *where neither moth or rust doth corrupt, and where thieves do not break through and steal."*

114

A man with assets of twelve and one half million dollars was converted. He read that command – *"Lay up treasures in Heaven,"* and thought within himself, "How can I convert all my holdings in oil, cattle, land, stocks and bonds into a treasure in Heaven?" He thought further, "Are cattle going to Heaven?" "No," was the answer. "Will oil go to heaven?" "No," was the answer. Then what goes to Heaven? Boys and girls, men and women go to Heaven. He then began to convert his physical holdings into cash and disperse the money into mission work, building church buildings, helping Bible colleges, and into every Christian work, which would help get men saved or which would prepare men for the work of the gospel.

Many years passed and a white haired old man smiled as he pressed his head to his dying pillow and said, "I did it!" "I did it!" " I have successfully converted all my oil, my cattle, and my stocks and bonds into spiritual dividends. All my earthly wealth has been converted into treasures in Heaven." With that, he went to be with his treasures.

I.   THERE ARE TWO OPTIONS FOR INVESTMENT

A.   This world's system.

1.   **Jesus said,** *"You are in the world, but you are not of the world"* (John 17:14-17).

2.   *"Seek those things which are above ... set your affections on things above, not on things on the Earth ... when Christ shall appear, then shall ye also appear with Him in glory"* (to be paid or rewarded for your work) (Colossians 3:1-4).

3.   *"Be not conformed* (become like) *to this world but be transformed by the renewing* (Studying the Bible to learn God's will and becoming more Christ-like) *of your mind."* (Romans 12:2).

B.   The world and all that is in it will be destroyed.

    1.   **Peter spoke of this event** in II Peter 3:10: *"The Earth also and the works that are in it, shall be burned up."*

    2.   **This age could end at any minute.** That's right. As these words are penned, there is no assurance that any new member will ever read them. Jesus MAY COME before that class is held. The Bible teaches that His coming is imminent. If He came tonight, the whole world system would go into the awesome great tribulational period. The world system would be destroyed.

C.   Which system are you going to invest in?

    1.   **One system** declares that there is no danger of losing one's investment. There is no thief that will steal, and there is no loss of value due to wear or deterioration. The smallest investment will be remembered and rewarded; i.e., a cup of cold water.

    2.   **Another system** will not survive. All investments will be completely lost or destroyed.

    3.   **Which company would a financial expert recommend?** A growing company with a bright future or one that is doomed to bankruptcy and total loss. The Financial Expert who made both companies advises and commands: *"But lay up for yourselves treasures in heaven, where neither moth nor rust doth corrupt, and where thieves do not break through nor steal"* (Matthew 6:20).

    4.   It is **your** money and **your** life! You have the power of decision. You will have to make the choice.

II.   PROSPERITY IS PROMISED TO THOSE WHO GIVE LIBERALLY

"Bring ye all the tithes into the storehouse, that there may be meat in mine house, and prove me now herewith, saith the Lord of hosts, IF I WILL NOT OPEN YOU THE WINDOWS of Heaven, and pour you out a blessing, that there shall not be room enough to receive it" (Malachi 3:10).

"Honor the Lord with thy substance, and with the firstfruits of all thine increase: SO SHALL THY BARNS BE FILLED with plenty, and thy PRESSES SHALL BURST OUT with new wine" (Proverbs 3:9-10).

"The liberal soul shall BE MADE FAT: and he that watereth shall be WATERED ALSO HIMSELF" (Proverbs 11:25).

"Give, and it shall be GIVEN UNTO YOU; good measure, pressed down, and shaken together, and running over, shall men give unto your bosom. For with the same measure ye mete, withal it shall BE MEASURED TO YOU AGAIN" (Luke 6:38).

"But this I say, He which SOWETH SPARINGLY shall reap also sparingly; and he which soweth bountifully shall reap also bountifully" (II Corinthians 9:6).

A.   God's Word promises financial prosperity.

If one would read these verses as he would a sales contract, or as he would a lease agreement, or as he would a legal, sworn document, he would believe. If he performed the first part of it, and met the first conditions, then he could claim the second part and expect the results promised.

B.   Read the Promises over again.

"Bring the tithes ... I will pour out a blessing and there will not be room enough to receive it." "Honor the Lord with thy substance ... first fruits ... barns

shall be filled ... presses burst out." "The liberal soul shall be made fat ... he that watereth shall be watered." "Give and it ... men shall give unto ... it shall be given unto you again."

We should face the Word of God honestly. God's Word promises financial prosperity to those who bring tithes and offerings. God not only gives financial prosperity to those who honor Him with their substance and with the firstfruits of their income, but He gives great peace and assurance to those who learn to make God a partner in material things. When one recognizes God's ownership of everything and gives tithes and offerings as a loving token of obedience, faith, and surrender, he enters into financial partnership with God. When this happens, he can claim the promise of Matthew 6:33, which promises, *"Seek ye first the kingdom of God and his righteousness and all these things shall be added unto you."* In the previous verses of the sixth chapter, Jesus illustrates how God takes care of the flowers and the birds that neither sow nor reap. He assures us that the believers are much more important than the flowers and birds and then promises, *"Seek ye first ... God will take care and supply all your needs!"* The author claimed the promise of this verse in 1950, and God has literally supplied all his needs ever since.

C.   God's pay is good.

Matthew 19:27-29 shows that God will pay 100% interest on some investments.   Think of what that means. 100% interest will be paid on the sacrificial decisions you make to follow the Lord and do HIS WILL!   What a paycheck many will have at the judgment seat of Christ!

III.   THE TEMPTATION NOT TO GIVE LIBERALLY...

The Devil works hard to prevent the Christian from giving to the Lord in a generous, systematic way.   There are several methods with which He confronts the child of God in order to prevent him from giving. If he can stop his giving, he can stop his growing. If he can stop the Christian's giving (sowing), he can stop the Christian's reaping and rejoicing! The most God-like characteristic the Christian develops is giving. The devil does not want the child of God to become GOD-LIKE. The Christian is commanded to be vigilant (watchful). He is to be watchful of his tempta-tions in the realm of giving.

A. Man's natural desire is to covet.

One does not have to teach a little boy to be selfish or to covet; it is his nature.

1. **Coveting is a respectable sin?** It is strange the way the sin of covetousness is considered by God's people. It is the respectable sin. It is the sin which strikes the deacon, the preacher, and the Sunday school teacher. The child of God who would never commit adultery, murder, or armed robbery thinks NOTHING OF COVET-ING.

2. **The sin of covetousness is best described as a Dr. Jekyl – Mr. Hyde sin.** To man it seems nice, acceptable, and a harmless practice. To God it is addicting, deferring from God's path, enslaving of one's will, alienating of one's love, and robbing of one's purpose.

3. **Coveting is a wicked sin.** Coveting is so dangerous, so wicked, so destructive to the individual, so dishonoring to God, that it is one of the sins of The Ten Commandments: *"Thou shall not murder, Thou shall not commit adultery, Thou shall not covet....* "Covetousness brought God's curse on Balaam (Numbers 22:21). Covetousness brought Leprosy upon Gehazi (II Kings 5:20). Covetousness of Aachan brought defeat to the army of Israel (Joshua 7). Covetousness brought death to Ananias and

Sapphira (Acts 5:1-10). Covetousness is the sin of idolatry (Colossians 3:5).

The church at Corinth (I Corinthians 5:11) was commanded to withdraw from a "brother" and not to keep company with a "brother" if he be a fornicator, or covetous, or a drunkard, or an extortioner – no, not to eat.

Coveting is behind all ungodly sin. The love of money causes all types of sin (I Timothy 6:10).

For the love of money, the bartender makes drunkards, paupers, and harlots out of people and damns their souls to Hell. For the love of money, the beautiful woman sells her body. For the love of money, every type of sin is committed under Heaven. God hates this sin of coveting. DO NOT be tempted to covet.

B. The natural tendency is to walk by sight.

Man loves to have faith as long as he can see where he is going. God commands tithing. He promises to bless and supply the need to those who tithe, yet man has a problem believing or trusting God, because he:

1. **Can't tithe because of all these bills.** "I just can't see how we can pay our bills if we started tithing."

2. **We'll start tithing when things get better.** "When I get my bills paid down where I can afford to tithe, I'd be happy to do it. I'll start then."

3. **I'm not going to give to that preacher.** There are many, who in looking for some excuse to justify not giving to God, find fault with the preacher. The child of God is to WALK BY FAITH, and TITHE BY FAITH. Do not be

tempted to offend God by calling God a liar through unbelief.

C. A natural tendency to doubt.

1. It won't do any good to tithe anyway.

2. That's what the old Jew said, *"It is vain to serve God, and what profit is it that we have kept his ordinance?"* (Malachi 3:14) The subject under consideration in this passage is giving. They said, "It doesn't do any good to give anyway."

3. The farmer plants his crops, but he doesn't expect to reap them the next day or the next week. God's laws are sure, one will reap what he sows (It might take some time or be at a later date). DO NOT doubt God. Give Him the first fruit, and HE will give the harvest at the proper time.

    One can overcome the sin of coveting by tithing. Overcome the sin of doubting by giving liberally. Overcome walking by sight by tithing by faith. God's cure for a stingy-selfish-coveting spirit is to accept the promises of God literally and then give, so He can honor his word by giving more back. *"Give and it shall be given ... He which soweth sparingly shall reap also sparingly; and he which soweth bountifully shall reap also bountifully"* (II Corinthians 9:6).

IV. TITHING IS TAUGHT THROUGHOUT THE BIBLE

"And of all that thou shalt give me I will surely give the tenth unto thee" (Genesis 28:22).

"And all the tithe of the land, whether of the seed of the land, or the fruit of the tree, is the Lord's: it is holy unto the Lord" (Leviticus 27:30).

The dictionary defines the tithe thusly: "To pay or give a tenth part of." In the Handy Dictionary of the Bible,

Merrill C. Tenney, the following is said concerning the tithe: a tenth part of one's income set aside for a specific use—to the government or ecclesiastics. Its origin is unknown, but it goes far beyond the time of Moses, and it was practiced in the lands from Babylonia to Rome. Abraham gave tithes to Melchizedek (Genesis 14:20; Hebrews 7:2, 6). Jacob promised tithes to God (Genesis 28:22).

A. Tithing was taught before the law.

1. **Ancient times.** Most scholars believe that the language used concerning Abel demonstrated that he tithed. We know he brought offerings.

2. **Abraham tithed.**

   "And blessed be the most high God, which hath delivered thine enemies into thy hand. And he gave him tithes of all" (Genesis 14:20; Hebrews 7:2, 6).

3. **Jacob tithes 400 years before Moses lived.**

   Jacob made a covenant with God saying, *"And this stone which I have set for a pillar shall be God's house, and of all that thou shalt give me, I will surely give a tenth unto thee"* (Genesis 28:22).

B. Tithing was incorporated into the law.

1. All Israelites were commanded to tithe (Leviticus 27:30-33).

2. The tithe was used to support the Levites and the temple service (Numbers 18:21-32).

3. Additional tithes were required at times (Deuteronomy 12:5-18; 14:22-29).

4. There were penalties charged for cheating on their tithes (Leviticus 27:31).

5. The Pharisees tithed on even herbs: *"Woe unto you, scribes and Pharisees, hypocrites! for ye pay tithe of mint and anise and cummin, and have omitted the weightier [matters] of the law, judgment, mercy, and faith"* (Matthew 23:23).

6. The tithe in the Old Testament acknowledged and glorified God.

7. Every Christian should tithe. B. H. Hillard gave a summary of Malachi 3:8-12 as follows:

   a. **Scriptural**: *"Bring YE all the tithe...."* God has never relinquished His claim on the tithe as the minimum of one's gift.

   b. **Simple**: *"Bring...."* Yes, just as simple as coming to church and bringing the tithe; just as a parent bringing a child. To "bring" implies complete control; coercive subjugation.

   c. **Serviceable**: *"Into the storehouse...."* The church is God's storehouse, into which all the tithe is to be brought; none of which is diverted through extraneous channels.

   d. **Sufficient**: *"That there may be meat in mine house."* *"Meat"* means a sufficiency for every need; wherein, under any circumstances, the tithe did fail to meet the requirements, God will make provision for that which is lacking.

   e. **Sublime**: *"Prove me now herewith...."* *"Prove me"* means to give God a chance. To use a slang phrase, it means "to put God on the spot." It is accepting God's challenge. God yearns for a chance to bless His people; and that chance comes when we accept God's challenge.

f. **Sensible**: *"If I will not open unto you the windows of Heaven, and pour you out a blessing that there shall not be room enough to receive it."* Common intelligence coupled with faith would lead one to tithe as the means of claiming such a promise. No person can believe this promise and fail to tithe. It would be unthinkable. Believe— tithe. Disbelieve— fail to tithe. There is no alternative.

g. **Satisfying**: *"And all nations shall call you blessed, for ye shall be a delightsome land"* (Malachi 3:12).

C. Jesus practiced tithing.

1. He fulfilled the law (Matthew 5:17-18).

2. He commended tithing (Matthew 23:23; Luke 11:42).

3. Jesus practiced what He preached.

D. Paul taught that the New Testament ministry was to be supported in the same manner as was the Levitical ministry.

1. **Paul, teaching on giving**.

a. Does a soldier pay his own salary while in the army (I Corinthians 9:7)?

b. Does a farmer plant grapes and not eat of the grapes (verse 7)?

c. Does a herdsman not partake of the flock (verse 7)?

d. Does an ox not eat of the corn (verse 9)?

2. **The spiritual realm of giving.**

He said that everyone who worked in a physical realm was a partaker of the fruit of his labor. Then He applied the same principle to the spiritual realm. He stated in Verse 11, *"If we have sown unto you spiritual things, is it a great thing if we shall reap your carnal [material] things?"*

3. **His illustration of supporting the ministry.**

In verse 13, he asks them if they were not aware of how the Levites were supported. *"They who wait [serve] at the alter are partakers with the alters."* The Bible clearly teaches that the alter workers, temple workers, and priests were supported by the tithes and offerings of the Jewish people.

4. **His statement on the standard of giving.**

a. In verse 14, he begins with the expression, *"Even so"*. This expression, *"Even so"* comes from the Greek "Houtos Kai." This is the same word found in John 3:14. As Moses lifted up the serpent in the wilderness, even so (Houtos Kai) must the Son of man be lifted up.

b. *"Houtos Kai"* means in the same manner or in the manner previously described.

c. Paul's point is that the standard that was used of God to support the Old Testament priest and temple workers is the same standard he ordained to support *"They who preach the gospel."* The standard *"Tithe and offerings."*

d. The literal statement of verse 14 is *"Even so"* [Houtos Kai]. In the manner previously described or illustrated in verse 13, *"Even so hath the Lord ordained that they which preach the gospel should live* (to be cared for) *of the gospel."*

E. **Let a man give as he purposeth in his heart** (II Corinthians 9:7).

This is a fine standard to use when a person will let the Bible help him to set the standard.

1. Paul was a Jew writing to a church (Church of Corinth), which was started in a Jewish synagogue and was made up of Jewish converts who were familiar with tithing (Acts 18:1-8).

2. The first example of a man purposing in his heart was Jacob. Jacob purposed to give back to God a tenth part or a tithe (Genesis 28:22).

V. **GOD WANTS YOU TO GIVE OF YOUR LIFE SO HE CAN REWARD YOU DURING THE MILLENNIAL REIGN (ETERNITY).**

A. The reason one should give to God is to express love and gratitude to God. God gave Jesus, His Son, health and all the materials and spiritual blessings of life. One expresses his love and appreciation when he gives back to God.

B   Giving back to God is one of His methods, which causes spiritual growth in the believer. *"It is more blessed to give then to receive."*

C. One can have rewards waiting for himself in Heaven, which will give him eternal blessings IF HE WILL GIVE TO GOD. Let Him reward you and multiply you FOR IT. *"He which soweth bountifully shall reap bountifully." (II Corinthians 9:6).*

GIVING

Monday
(Introduction – Options for Investment)

1. Lay not up for yourselves treasure upon _____ (Matthew 6:19).

2. How did the millionaire convert his holdings into the spiritual dividends? _____ _____ _____ _____ _____.

3. You are in the world, but you are _____ of the _____ (John 17:14).

4. Which system will not survive? _____ _____ (II Peter 3:10).

5. When Paul said, *"Be not conformed to this world"* (Romans 12:2), what did he mean? _____ _____

6. Which system would be the wise system to invest in? _____ _____ _____ (Matthew 5:19-20).

Tuesday
(Prosperity Promised)

1. What would a person have to do to secure the promise: "Pour you out a blessing ... shall not be room enough to contain it." _____ (Malachi 3:10).

2. What does God promise the person who will honor the Lord with his first fruits? _____ _____ _____ (Proverbs 3:9)

3. The liberal soul shall be _____ _____ (Proverbs 11:25).

4. Give, and it shall be _____ _____ _____; shall men give unto your bosom. (Luke 6:38).

5. He which soweth _____ shall reap _____, and he who sows _____ shall reap bountifully. (II Corinthians 9:6).

6. Are these promises of God literal or should we not believe them? They _____ _____.

Wednesday
(Temptation Not to Give)

1. Our natural desire is to _____.

2. One of the most God-like characteristics _____ _____ _____ _____ _____.

3. What sin is the child of God most likely to commit? The sin of _____.

4. What does God think of the sin of coveting? He _____ it.

5. What sin caused the death of Achan, Ananias and Sapphira? _____ _____ _____ _____.

Thursday
(Tithing is Taught)

1. What is the religious definition of "tithe"? _____
   _____ _____ _____ _____.

2. Was tithing taught before the law? Give an example.
   _____.

3. Give the seven steps in Mr. Hillard's summary of Malachi
   3:8-12. 1._____ 2._____
   3._____ 4._____ 5._____
   6._____ 7._____

4. Give the Scripture where Jesus commended tithing.
   _____ _____:_____

5. Jacob gave tithes about _____ years before the law was
   given by Moses.

6. Give a Scripture, which commanded the Jews to tithe while
   under the Law of Moses. _____ _____:_____

Friday
(Paul Teaching on Giving)

1. Give an example that shows that one is to partake of the
   fruit of his labors. _____ _____.

2. Paul said if we sow unto your spiritual things we should
   reap from your _____ things. (I Corinthians 9:11).

3. How were the Levites (temple workers) supported? By
   _____ and _____.

4. What does the expression "Houtos Kai" mean?

   _____ _____ _____.

5. God wants us to give liberally so we can _____
   something when we _____ to _____.

Having studied this lesson on giving, I now understand that the reason God commands His children to give tithes and offerings is so that they may grow spiritually, and that they may have treasures in Heaven when they get there. I now purpose in my heart to give liberally and systematically of my tithes and offerings. In doing this I will not only help support the work, which has greatly blessed me, but will follow the design, plan of spiritual growth, and of laying up treasures in Heaven.

_____ _____
                Name   Date

Questions to ask my discipler:

DAILY DECLARATION

Repeat Aloud Each Morning and Evening

The promises of God concerning the blessings received from giving are just as true as all of His other promises.

MEMORY VERSE: *"Give, and it shall be given unto you; good measure, pressed down, and shaken together, and running over, shall men give into your bosom. For with the same measure that ye mete withal it shall be measured to you again"* (Luke 6:38).

CHECK BLOCK AFTER REPEATING

	Mon	Tues	Wed	Thurs	Fri	Sat	Sun
A.M.							
P.M.							

TEN COMMANDMENTS FOR THE ROLE MODEL

I. **THOU SHALT** ACCEPT THY SACRED TRUST AS A DISCIPLE. Jesus commanded, disciple all nations (Matt. 28:19).

II. **THOU SHALT** SERVE AS AN EXTENTION OF YOUR PASTOR. Mention the pastor's love and concern for the family often.

III. **THOU SHALT** GUARD YOUR INFLUENCE AT ALL TIMES. Your life must be in complete harmony with your purpose of strengthening your disciple.

IV. **THOU SHALT NOT** ATTEMPT TO IMPRESS YOUR DISCIPLE with your knowledge, but at all times try to further his.

V. **THOU SHALT** PRAY REGULARLY FOR YOUR NEW CHRISTIAN and his family, calling them and their needs by name.

VI. **THOU SHALT** SIT WITH HIM IN CHURCH, and introduce him to other good solid Christians, which can aid his spiritual growth.

VII. **THOU SHALT** BE FAITHFUL TO THE WEEKLY MEETING IN HIS HOME, and be constantly alert of ways to encourage him.

VIII. **THOU SHALT** WORK TO ENROLL HIM IN THE REGULAR SERVICES: Sunday School, prayer meeting, and out-reach.

IX. **THOU SHALT** NOTIFY THE PASTOR AT ONCE when you are confronted with a problem which needs his pastoral care.

X. **THOU SHALT** CONTINUE TO ENCOURAGE AND EDIFY your new Christian after your period of discipleship has expired.

Lesson No. 10

THE TORCH IS PASSED

II Timothy 2:2

INTRODUCTION: In the ancient Olympic games much was made of passing the eternal flame to a new generation of contestants who were eager to perform before the waiting masses. But the flame was NOT ETERNAL, and all their great performances, their great achievements, and their daring feats will soon be forgotten FOREVER.

But there is something which one can pass which will NEVER BE FORGOTTEN and ITS GLORY WILL NEVER FADE!

Daniel the prophet spoke of the SOUL WINNER: *"And they that be wise shall shine as the brightness of the firmament; and they that turn many to righteousness as the stars for ever and ever"* (Daniel 12:3). They that are WISE and he that WINNETH SOULS **is as shining as the brightness of the firmament and the stars FOREVER AND EVER.** But, there is much more in Daniel 12:3 than winning souls. There is the Discipleship Program and also "the follow-up" for new converts.

LOOK! "...*they that TURN MANY TO RIGHTEOUSNESS"* That means righteous living, which means discipling.

Now, what is the reward for winning them, discipling, developing, or turning many to righteousness?

They will shine as the stars forever and ever. That means eternal rewards, eternal glory for winning and developing souls.

I.   YOUR PERSONAL COMMISSION FROM PAUL

A.   The child of God has a personal commission from Paul.

It is a commission to teach what one has been taught. Paul told Timothy, *"And the things that thou hast heard of me* (the things Paul taught Timothy) *among many witnesses, the same* (what Paul taught) *commit* (teach) *thou to FAITHFUL MEN, who (FAITHFUL MEN) shall be able to teach others also,"* (II Timothy 2:2).

1. **There are four responsible teachers** in that verse:

    a. Paul who taught Timothy,

    b. Timothy who taught faithful men,

    c. Faithful men who taught others, and

    d. Others.

2. **What were the others to do?** It is inferred that they should begin the circle of teaching all over again. This revolving circle of one generation teaching another generation has finally reached YOU. You have been shown some truths, which you are now under solemn obligation to teach others ALSO!

3. **I Peter 3:15 and the Great Commission.** In 1 Peter 3:15, Peter boldly states that the child of God is to: *"and [be] ready always to [give] an answer to every man that asketh you."* The Great Commission to the church commands *"Go ye therefore, and teach all nations"* (Matthew 28:18-20). Thus, the child of God's duty of teaching others is clearly commanded in the Bible.

B. **They still act like visitors.**

There are so many in churches who, although they have been there for months, if not years, are still demanding to be served and ministered to. They conduct themselves as guests instead of members of the Household of Faith. Are you one of those who is still acting like a visitor?

1. **I'm just new to the Faith**.

    There are multitudes of people who have been saved for years which are still babes in Christ. The author was talking to a man who kept saying, "I'm just a young Christian." We would talk a while longer, and he would say, "I'm just a young Christian." He evidently felt embarrassed, because of his lack of knowledge of God's word, and he excused himself by telling me, "I'm new to the Faith. I'm just a young Christian."

    Finally, the author asked him, "How long have you been saved?" His shocking answer was "Eight years."

    The **angels** wept in heaven!
    The **sun** turned its head in shame!
    The **birds** stopped their singing!

    And if one could have heard it, there was a groan which escaped from the lips of Jesus.

    Eight years old and still a babe in Christ, still on the bottle, and still untrained.

2. **The Book of Acts**.

    When one reads the Book of Acts, he finds 3,000 saved and added to the 120 (Acts 2:42). In a few days, one finds these new converts going from house to house teaching. In the next few years, their number had swelled to well over 100,000 members. Many of them gave their lives as martyrs. They were strong in the Faith.

    In Acts 19, one finds twelve disciples. These twelve, along with all their converts, evangelized the whole province of Asia in the space of two years. From lost sinners, to babes in Christ, to flaming evangelists; ALL IN TWO SHORT YEARS. The Book of Ephesians, written to them later, proves that they were mature Christians.

3. **Pray tell, what is the difference?** Today there are many who confess that they are still babes in Christ after being saved for years. In the New Testament days, the disciples became flaming evangelists and evangelized their whole area in two short years (Acts 19:10).

C. Down on the Farm

1. **Doing a day's work.**

Many of the older people, people who were raised on a farm, can remember when kids 10-12 years old were doing a man's job. They would work right along side of their bigger brothers in the field from morning to night. It was what was expected of them while they were growing up. One generation was expected to work and was taught to work. The next generation was left in a world of television and idleness and was not expected or taught to work. The first generation was milking cows before growing big enough to reach up to the "faucet" and give the appropriate squeeze. The second generation was still acting like babies.

2. Many today grow up and never learn how to work. Recently, in a nation-wide poll, it was revealed that there were college graduates who were not trained well enough to hold down a job. It is shocking to learn of college graduates who do not know how to work, who can't find a job.

3. What is the difference in the two generations of "kids."

a. Is it the "kids"? NO!!

      b.   It is the parents and the training the parents give their children.

D. Which Pattern are you going to follow?

1. **Are you going to follow** the book of Acts' pattern of being a mature, spirit-filled, soul-winning Christian in a few short months?

2. **Will you be like the man** who was eight years old and still on a bottle and still whining around like a baby?

3. **Will you work like they did,** or will you live like those on our modern day welfare rolls who do not have the motivation to work or serve Christ?

II. THE MISTAKE ILLUSTRATED

A. What has happened?

One may wonder how things got into the shape they are in. The following story will illustrate the problem.

B. The case of poor penmanship.

A little boy had been repeatedly warned by the teacher to use more care and to take greater pains in using proper penmanship when writing. Finally, the teacher had to take corrective measures.

She said, "Johnny, you are going to have to stay after school and write this sentence 100 times on the blackboard."

She wrote the sentence on the blackboard.

The model sentence was done in beautiful penmanship.

Each letter was formed precisely.

The bell rang, school was over, and Johnny began his long task of writing the long sentence 100 times. The first few sentences were beautiful.

Johnny looked often to the model in order to get the letters formed just right, but alas, HIS FINAL SENTENCE WAS BARELY LEGIBLE.

What was his problem? Where was his failure? What went wrong?

Johnny had looked at the example directly above the line he was writing instead of referring back to the original model, which the teacher had given him as an example.

Alas, our problem! Many have been looking at the sloppy examples of careless, untrained Christians who looked at the sloppy examples of others before them instead of looking back and seeing THE PERFECT EXAMPLE IN THE BOOK OF ACTS.

III. PAYING FOR YOUR "RAISIN."

A. Another country-fide expression.

The old timers used to say, "The only way one can pay for his 'raisin' is to raise some 'young-uns' of his own."

- **If** YOU have enjoyed these lessons;
- **If** YOU have and grown spiritually because of them,
- **If** YOU have prospered and found your place in the church family, because of this DISCIPLE-SHIP PROGRAM AND YOUR DISCIPLIER, and
- **If** YOU would like to show your appreciation and say an appropriate THANK YOU to your church and pastor;

YOU can do all this and repay your DISCIPLIER for all that he has done for you by "RAISIN" SOME "YOUNG-UNS" YOURSELF! There is another new convert coming along who needs a DISCIPLIER just like you.

That old time country saying, you can only pay for your "raisin" by raising some yourself is true spiritually. You show your love, your appreciation, your thankfulness by teaching, developing and serving others. There is someone who needs your help. You are someone's Big Brother. He is looking up to you and needs your love, encouragement, and help. If you desire to continue your spiritual growth and have the joy of the Lord, then the next step in your Christian life is to help disciple others.

If **they were expected to do it** in THE BOOK OF ACTS, and **they did it** in THE BOOK OF ACTS, then God **expects you to do it** NOW! and **YOU CAN DO IT!!!**

Monday

(Introduction)

1. In the ancient Olympic games much was made of passing the _____ _____.
2. The flame was not _____ and their daring feats will soon be forgotten.
3. Daniel spoke of the reward of the soul-winner in Daniel ____:____ .
4. *"He that winneth souls is _____."*
5. There will be _____ rewards for winning and _____ souls.

Tuesday

(Your Personal Commission)

1. It is a commission to _____ what you have been _____ .
2. There are _____ responsible teachers in the verse ___ _____ ____:____ .
3. This revolving circle of one _____ teaching _____ generation has finally reached _____.
4. Be ____ ____ always to give an _____ to _____ man that asketh you.
5. Our duty of _____ _____ is clearly commanded in the Bible.

Wednesday
(Are You Still Acting?)

1. Are you still _____ like a visitor?
2. They conduct themselves as _____ instead of _____ of the family.
3. Eight years old and still a _____ in Christ, still on the _____, still _____.
4. _____ members to _____ added in Acts 2:42 to well over _____ in a few short years.
5. From _____sinners to _____ in Christ, to flaming _____ all in the space of _____ years.

Thursday
(Down on The Farm)

1. On the farm kids _____ years old were doing a _____ job.
2. It is shocking to learn that some _____ graduates do not know how _____ _____.
3. What is the _____ in the two generations of _____?
4. Is the difference in the kids? _____.
5. Will you work like they did _____ on the _____, or will you live like some who do not have motivation or the _____ to really _____ or _____ Christ.

141

Friday

(Our Mistake Illustrated)

1. The case of poor _____.

2. What was his _____? Where was his _____?

3. We have been looking at _____ examples instead of the examples in the Book of Acts.

4. The only way you can _____ for your _____ is to raise some _____-_____of your own.

5. There is another _____ _____ who needs a

   _____.

6. If they _____ it in the Book of Acts, then God expects _____ ___ ___ it _____.

Having studied this book and found how easy it is to learn the simple truths of God's Word, I now am ready to continue to go further in my studies in a more advanced series of lessons. I further desire to "Help pay for my "raisin" by helping a NEW CONVERT as the pastor may direct.

_____ _____
Name   Date

NOTE: Read the "My Ten Declarations To True Discipleship" on the next page.

DAILY DECLARATION

Read aloud each morning and evening

MY TEN DECLARATIONS TO TRUE DISCIPLESHIP

Having completed the past ten lessons, **I now understand** that God saved me FOR A DEFINITE PURPOSE. Therefore, I will do my best in the following areas as a true disciple of Christ.

I will strive to accept each trial or problem in life as a stepping stone to a CLOSER WALK WITH CHRIST (I Peter 5:10; II Corinthians 4:17; I Corinthians 10:13).

1. **I will read and study the bible** EACH DAY (II Timothy 2:15; Psalms 119:11).
2. **I will strive** to be FAITHFUL TO THE REGULAR SER-VICES of my church (Hebrews 10:25).
3. **I will** HONOR, SUBMIT TO, and FOLLOW the leadership of my Pastor (Hebrews 13:7; 13:17).
4. **I will be** REGULAR IN MY PRAYER LIFE and will PRAY SPECIFICALLY for the requests on my prayer list (I Thessalonians 5;17; Matthew 7:7-8).
5. **I will return** TO CHRIST MY LORD a tenth of my income and will share liberally as the Lord may direct (II Corinthians 9:6-14).
6. **I will accept my responsibility** to WORLD WIDE EVAN-GELISM as the Lord may direct (John 20:21; Acts 1:8).
7. **I will strive** to live my life in the light of the SOON COMING OF THE LORD JESUS CHRIST (John 14:3; Mark 13:34-37; Revelation 20:12).
8. **I will strive** to be wise and follow the most Christ-like examples of discipleship and WIN SOULS IN MY DAILY LIFE (Proverbs 11:30; I Corinthians 19:22).
9. **I will make these declarations**, TRUSTING IN THE GRACE OF GOD to enable me to have strength to keep them (Philippians 4:19).

_____   _____
Name   Date

MEMORY VERSES: *I beseech you therefore, brethren, by the mercies of God, that ye present your bodies a living sacrifice, holy, acceptable unto God, [which is] your reasonable service. And be not conformed to this world: but be ye transformed by the renewing of your mind, that ye may prove what [is] that good, and acceptable, and perfect, will of God* (Romans 12:1-2).

What? know ye not that your body is the temple of the Holy Ghost [which is] in you, which ye have of God, and ye are not your own? For ye are bought with a price: therefore glorify God in your body, and in your spirit, which are God's (I Corinthians 6:19-20).

CHECK BLOCK AFTER REPEATING

	Mon	Tues	Wed	Thurs	Fri	Sat	Sun
A.M.							
P.M.							

Questions to ask my discipler:

IN BEHALF OF OUR LORD AND SAVIOR JESUS CHRIST
AND OUR BELOVED CHURCH
WE HEARTILY CONGRATULATE AND COMMEND

OUR NEW CONVERT

FOR OUTSTANDING WORK IN COMPLETING THIS SERIES IN

CHRISTIAN GROWTH

We are grateful for the fine way you have grown
spiritually and found your place in our church family.

_____   _____
Your Discipler   Your Pastor

NEW CONVERT CARE DISCIPLESHIP PROGRAM

These booklets and books are presented to help the layman in the local church. We are dedicated to aiding the Pastor in strengthening members. Through the New Convert Care Discipleship Program, we help new converts become happy, active parts of the church family.

Through the Layman Library Series, we present books designed to train and strengthen. **Please contact author for prices.**

THE LAYMAN LIBRARY SERIES

OTHER BOOKS BY DR. WILKINS

Dr. James Wilkins, Director
New Testament Ministries
P.O. Box 291,
Bedford, Texas 76095
(817) 267-6239; E-mail: Pwilkins96@aol.com